TOM BRUCE

SILENT GRIEF

SILENT GRIEF

Living in the Wake of Suicide

CHRISTOPHER LUKAS

&

HENRY M. SEIDEN, PH.D.

Charles Scribner's Sons   New York

Charles Scribner's Sons
Macmillan Publishing Company
866 Third Avenue, New York, NY 10022
Collier Macmillan Canada, Inc.

Library of Congress Cataloging-in-Publication Data

Lukas, Christopher.
    Silent grief.

    Bibliography: p.
    Includes index.
    1. Suicide—United States. 2. Bereavement—Psychological
aspects.   I. Seiden, Henry M., 1940–
II. Title.
HV6548.U5L85   1987   362.2   87-23328

ISBN 0-684-18770-1

Macmillan books are available at special discounts for bulk
purchases for sales promotions, premiums, fund-raising, or
educational use. For details, contact:

Special Sales Director
Macmillan Publishing Company
866 Third Avenue
New York, NY 10022

10 9 8 7 6 5 4 3 2 1

Printed in the United States of America

To E.S.L.—
may she now rest in peace—and S.R.L.,
whose idea this book was

Silence is no certain token
That no secret grief is there;
Sorrow which is never spoken
Is the heaviest load to bear.
—FRANCES RIDLEY HAVERGAL

Contents

CONTENTS

Part Three: Giving Help and Getting Help
Listening and Talking

Acknowledgments

Over the course of the years it took to research and write this book there have been many people who helped, people who offered their insight and suggestions. Among those who provided such help we must thank the following:

The New Jersey Self-Help Clearing House, Ed Madara, director, for pointing us in the direction of a number of groups and the whole self-help movement; the group at Saint Ann's Guild Room in Brooklyn, for their understanding of our need to spend time with them; Hal and Debbie Cohen, for their aid with our word processors; the Center for Preventive Psychiatry; Westchester Jewish Community Services; The American Association of Suicidology; our persevering agent, Christine Tomasino. Finally, our wives, Susan and Sara, without whom we never would have accomplished this project.

WHAT SURVIVORS SAY

I've had a lot of deaths in the family, but never something like this.

Suicide cheats us out of time to say good-bye.

The extra problem of suicide survivors is our feeling that if we'd only done something different, if we'd only made him feel more loved, he'd be alive today. What did we do wrong?

I had no chance to say "I'm sorry."

I keep dreaming I have another chance to save her!

It's the suddenness of it all that makes the difference.

My nephew killed himself. Since then his widow has gotten stomach problems, his sister has an ulcer, his twin brother attempted suicide, and his best friend became a gambler and got divorced.

You come away feeling there isn't much you can do, you're helpless.

I feel guilty about feeling relieved.

I feel vulnerable. I'm afraid it will happen to others in our family.

Why? Why? Why?

Part One

___

THE SHORT TERM
"What's Happening to Me?"

Introduction

LUKAS'S STORY

On a hot August afternoon in 1941, when I was six years old, and she was thirty-three, my mother walked out of her psychiatrist's house in Connecticut, stepped into the garden, and cut her throat. My father, a successful lawyer—though an unhappy man—was summoned from his New York office to deal with the death. Also at the psychiatrist's house that day was my grandmother. She had been taking my mother to the psychiatrist that summer; the visits were the culmination of years of manic-depressive bouts. There was some disagreement between my mother's mother and my father on what to tell the children—me, at home, and my eight-year-old brother, away at camp. My father won the argument: For ten years the nature of my mother's death was kept a secret from us, though all our relatives and most of their friends knew that she had committed suicide.

When I was finally told the truth, at the age of sixteen, my father and I were sitting in a railroad station on another hot August day. I was about to catch a train, and I have always believed that my father chose that moment to tell me because he could not bear to hold a prolonged conversation on the subject. "Why?" I querulously inquired. "She was sick," my father replied, making it clear that was all he had to say on the subject. We didn't talk about it again for many years.

Twenty-nine years later, after my father's death (he was an alcoholic; his liver gave out), and after success in dealing with my own relative depressions and anxieties (in and out of psychotherapy), an aging aunt and uncle also killed themselves, a year apart. He—my mother's brother—had also been manic-depressive. My aunt had cancer. I was asked to speak at both their memorial services. To my dismay, I found that I was extremely angry: at them, at what they had done to their children and to me, at my cousins for asking me to speak. But I also found myself feeling guilty, because I was angry at two dead people. At the memorial services no mention was made of suicide. My aunt and uncle had simply been taken by Death.

After some consideration, it occurred to me that my rage and guilt were connected to my mother's death years before. Perhaps I needed to explore that connection. Perhaps I would—someday.

Then, four years ago, my closest childhood friend turned fifty and, simultaneously, killed himself. He was the boy judged "most likely to succeed" in our class at high school. I had lost track of him over the years, though occasional reports had filtered through to me from the town out West where he had settled: He had had one bad marriage and one good one; his alcoholism was under control; he was doing some writing. My reaction to his death was great despondency. It was now imperative that I explore my feelings further.

My wife suggested I turn to the literature of suicide. With all the current attention to people killing themselves, perhaps there I could find solace; perhaps I might even find some practical help. I found neither. Of some twenty-two hundred works on suicide that had been published since 1965—books, articles, reports in professional journals, theses—only a handful even mentioned the effects of suicide upon survivors. Most of the scholarly works and most of the research dealt with the person who kills himself. The popular press likewise almost never concerned itself with those left behind. It stressed the rash of adolescent deaths, "rational" suicide, epidemics of depression.

Still, between the lines, in a few pieces of literature, here and there, I began to uncover some startling facts. If you are reading this book because you, too, are the survivor of a suicide by someone close to you, then some of these facts may be familiar. If you are not, they may be strikingly new.

The Numbers

For every person who successfully commits suicide, it is estimated that there are seven to ten people intimately affected: parents, siblings, children, aunts, uncles, grandparents, grandchildren, close friends. If we accept the official United States Health Department suicide toll of approximately 30,000 people a year, that means that between 200,000 and 300,000 people become suicide survivors each year. If, on the other hand, we take the more likely (unofficial) figure of over 60,000 suicides a year (a percentage of automobile accidents, drug overdoses, alcohol-related deaths, suicides that are covered up by relatives and coroners), then the numbers become larger—between 350,000 and 600,000 new survivors are created each year. Assuming that most of those people remain living for another fifteen to twenty years, I came up with the staggering notion that, conservatively, there are 6 million people now living in this country who are survivors of a suicide by someone close to them. Maybe more.

The Problems

Among the things my reading showed was that while many relatives of people who die "normal" deaths suffer shock, denial, or helplessness as a result of those deaths (in addition to grief or sadness), the survivor of a suicidal death apparently suffers more: guilt, anger (bordering on rage), and pain—feelings that go on for years. In addition, the survivor may experience exhaustion, migraines, colitis, alcoholism, sleep problems, anxieties, crying spells, heart trouble, and fear of being alone. Survivors use more tranquilizers and have more ulcers and more depression. Finally, and most tragically, as a group they are more likely to have difficulty with lasting relationships and more likely to commit suicide themselves than is the general population. No wonder that Edwin Shneidman, the founder of the American Association for Suicidology, started using the term *survivor/victim* to refer to those left behind.

But as I tried to dig deeper into the literature, I came up dry. The problems encountered by suicide survivors were only hinted at. There was so little research that no one could say definitively that this result was or was not so, that this fact had been proved. And yet, the material I read made sense to me; it resonated with my own experience with suicide. I was filled with questions.

Why did all this happen?

What were people doing about it?

Why did the survivor suffer so?

How did the long list of ailments relate to my own problems?

Why, despite the available evidence that suicide survivors go through something especially difficult ("It is well documented," one psychologist said to me, "that survivors are deeply affected, even years later"), is there so little public notice or written material?

And why, in the more than forty years since my mother's death, did no one ever say to me that what I was going through was part of what most suicide survivors experience? It would have helped.

It seemed to me that some of us who have gone through such painful experiences should talk about them; we should share our lives with others. I decided to write a book on the subject, one that would lay out for survivors and for the general population the dimension of the problem, the effects upon those left behind, and—if possible— what could be done for them. I started interviewing people who had been left behind, talking to psychologists and social workers, going through more of the psychological literature. Early on, in 1983, I attended a conference—billed as the first get-together of suicide survivors—convened by the University of Medicine and Dentistry of the New Jersey Community Mental Health Center of Rutgers Medical School. There, some one hundred survivor/victims of suicide (many recently so) recounted the angers, guilts, and anxieties of being left behind. From those whose pain was of longer duration (months and years), it seemed clear that, though time might soften the outward appearance of trauma, there were many, many problems for survivors that lasted.

The book, then, would be about people who had suffered through the suicide of a loved one, about what they had learned, and about what they were still trying to learn of the strange event that threatened to destroy their lives.

A WORD ABOUT APPROACH

As I dug deeper and deeper into the effects of suicide upon survivors, I realized that I needed someone with professional expertise to help me. I asked Henry Seiden, a long-time practitioner of psychoanalytic psychotherapy, to write the book with me. The material in the book is, in general, derived from our joint thinking and research.

We have broken the book into a number of categories. They contain information on suicide, on reactions to suicide, and on the problems with which survivor/victims have had to struggle. Equally important, they also contain the stories of many people whom we have interviewed in an effort to get at the essence of what it means to be a suicide survivor. As with all victims (of robbery, rape, car accidents, attempted murder, torture, mugging), the survivors have something to learn and something to pass on. They are sons, daughters, parents, grandparents, grandchildren, best friends, lovers, siblings, and friends of people who have killed themselves. Their stories contain hope as well as despair, success as well as failure. In addition, we have talked with psychologists, social workers, therapists, and researchers, to summon up as much of the useful knowledge about the aftermath of suicide as we can.

During the three years that the book has been in the writing, there has been a small but gratifying increase in the number of psychologists and researchers who are paying attention to the suicide survivor. A second and a third Rutgers conference have taken place. Others are planned. Some preliminary scholarly research has cast some doubt on the presumed differences between suicide survivors and the survivors of any violent and sudden death, but everyone agrees that more research needs to be done, that massive conclusions about "the facts" are not yet warranted. What is clear to Henry Seiden and me, however, is that the people to whom we talked were suffering from very real pain. And many who had suffered the sudden (normal) death of other family members asserted vehemently that this survivorship was vastly different. (In fact, 97 percent of the respondents to one questionnaire said that death by suicide was more difficult to cope with than previous encounters with death.) But this book was never intended to be a scientific analysis. We set out to reflect talks with numerous survivors, to get their unvarnished feelings about what scars remained from the experience of having people close to them kill themselves.

There is no doubt in their minds, and there is no doubt in mine, that such survivors experience something qualitatively and quantitatively different from the experiences of survivors of natural and accidental deaths. We offer you the results of our conversations, and those that many others—across the country—have had with similar survivors.

One of the most painful things that came out of the talks with survivor/victims, whether they were still bound up in grief or whether they had gotten some perspective on their loss, was the realization that someone whom they had deeply cared about had chosen to leave them; not in an "everyday" fashion—by walking out or suing for divorce—but by death. Survivors are traumatized by the notion that someone has rejected them in this fashion. Shneidman himself has suggested that one of the reasons for the great pain survivors feel (and the anger it foments) is that they have to face the realization that the dead person "renounced all possibility of help from them." This leaves them feeling quite worthless.

Another startling realization, one that was at first puzzling, was how many people, men especially, had not discussed the suicide with family members even years after the event. (In this, as in so many things, I found I was not alone.) By not talking about it, survivors had often not been able to go through some of the normal healing processes. They were "frozen" in their grief. From my own experiences, and from what we have found in our investigations, there seems little doubt that a good deal of the special pain of the survivor/victim is due to this silence, a silence that is aided and abetted by the reluctance of society to discuss suicide at all. Why there is so much silence—why there is actually a family agreement not to talk—is the subject of chapter 11.

All of us who have suffered through a suicide have feelings that threaten to cripple us, though often we may not acknowledge them. Often, such feelings prevent us from finding our way through the maze of our lives. They become roadblocks. We call such roadblocks *bargains*. Chapters 4 through 11 deal with them and their consequences.

As I grew up and became aware of the nature of my mother's death,

I wanted to know more than whether her illness would be my fate as well (and that was a terrifying and recurring nightmare); more than whether my relatives, my children, would also kill themselves. I wanted to know *why.* In this book, we deal with silence, recriminations, why, and many of the other questions that plague us as survivor/victims.

WHO IS IN THIS BOOK AND HOW
THEY CAME TO BE HERE

My initial aim was to write a book that could help other survivors cope. But when Henry and I started to work together, we realized that by concentrating simply on coping we would be leaving out a large part of the survivor's story. In the end, we've tried to put down on paper the full gamut of the survivor's experience.

Who are these people? Among those we talked to personally, there is Ralph, whose father shot himself over fifty years ago. There is Amanda, whose daughter took an overdose. Erik, whose son jumped out a window; May, whose father hanged himself when she was only nine; Sean, whose father and two brothers all killed themselves. Included are a nurse, a doctor, a railroad employee, a social worker, several retired people, the manager of a department store, a young woman who works in a pharmacy, an apartment house superintendent, several schoolteachers, an unemployed accountant. There is a wide range in the amount of time since the suicide. The most distant is fifty-five years ago, the most recent, three months before our interview.

Almost every familial and extrafamilial relationship presented itself: There are sons and daughters, fathers and mothers, spouses and lovers, uncles and aunts. At least half of the people who had killed themselves had tried before; many, more than once. Of the survivors we talked to at length, over half were depressed or had psychological or physical problems that seemed to be related to their role as survivor. One of them admitted to having tried to kill herself; many of them had thought about it. We talked to more women than men; but a larger number of men than women were among the dead. (This fits the national statistics: More men complete the suicidal act; more survivors, therefore, are women.) Despite the large attention paid to adolescent suicide these days (about one-seventh of all suicides is estimated to be someone under twenty-one), we did not concentrate on any one kind of suicide or any one kind of survivor.

How did we find these people? Some came to us from local mental health centers where they had gone in search of help. Others we met at the Rutgers conference on suicide survivors. They agreed to meet afterward for extended talks. Occasionally, we would be talking about the book and someone would overhear and say, "Excuse me, I couldn't help hearing what you were talking about. My sister's husband killed himself and I'm sure she'd be anxious to talk to you about it." In fact, the most striking thing about people whom we talked to was how willing they were to talk. Sometimes, nearing the end of the audiotape, or looking at a watch and realizing that we had kept someone past his or her dinner (or bed) time, we would say, "Okay, thanks," and turn off the tape. Most people would go on talking. They didn't want to stop. Talking about suicide, about what it means to be a survivor, seemed to be something survivors were anxious to do.

This fits in with something we have heard over and over again from psychologists and that also makes common sense: It helps to talk. Of course, there were some people who were more eager to talk than others. Men, for instance, seemed to be less willing, or less needful, or thought they were. And there were others who, for one reason or another, couldn't bring themselves to open up this painful subject at all. But for the most part, that's how we got a good deal of the material we're passing on in this book: through old-fashioned conversations. And it bears repeating—contrary to general opinion, *survivors will talk about suicide if they are certain someone will listen.*

We also received newsletters and brochures from the small number of self-help survivor groups across the country; other information and ideas came from newspaper articles, professional journals, meetings, books—most of them about the person who commits suicide, but a few about survivors themselves. The New Jersey Self-Help Clearing House, run by Ed Madara, was a source of information, as were other mental health groups.

Henry Seiden and I shared the writing of this book. His expertise is in the area of mental health; mine is as a survivor. Together, we looked at the interviews and research from those points of view. Together, we puzzled out the dilemmas, sorted through the shattered lives, and tried to put together words of comfort to those who think that the future holds nothing but bleak days of depression. In that sense, this is a self-help book, one based on solid precepts of psychology.

But in the end, it is not what we say but what the survivors say that is likely to be the most helpful to readers. Most survivors, whether going through the tremors of a recent suicide or looking back at one over the years, feel alone. "We don't know what will happen next, and we don't know whom to talk to to find out or how to make the experience less lonely." Ironically, the conversations showed us that there is a great deal in common between survivors; that what one person experiences—both emotionally and in terms of events—is often similar to what another person experiences; that sharing with other survivors would help. The fact that we survivors don't believe that similarity, that we think, instead, that our pain, our problems, our lives, are unique, is part of the survivor's dilemma. The paradox, of course, is that every suicidal event, like the person involved, *is* unique. But as you will see, there is a deep family resemblance between all the survivors whose stories appear in this book. It is from those common threads that other survivors may be able to draw some lessons for their own lives, to help dispel the isolation, disorientation, despair, emptiness, and shame.

Every trauma leaves scars that get in the way of normal functioning. Physical trauma, caused by events such as automobile accidents, leave physical scars. Psychological trauma leave psychological scars. Suicide appears to leave its survivor/victims with both. This book is about the people who are survivors, about their scars, and about how to make them less damaging or—with luck—how to make them disappear.

This book is written for two kinds of people: (a) for survivors who want to learn more about the survivor's experience and about how to change their lives for the better; and (b) for anyone else who wishes to understand what survivors go through.

To a large extent, this book would not exist if it were not for the people who shared their stories and their feelings with us. They hope, as do I, that their insights and their experiences, even their painful

11

ones, will be of help to the hundreds of thousands who are added to the list of survivor/victims every year.

—*Christopher Lukas*

A NOTE TO THE READER

From time to time we quote from other people's writings. All attributions and credits appear in a single section at the end of this book, along with a short bibliography.

Because most people we interviewed wished to remain anonymous, we have changed their names.

Chapter 1

WHAT HAPPENS TO THE SURVIVOR AFTER SOMEONE COMMITS SUICIDE

In most cultures and in most periods of history the attitude to suicide has had something in common with that to homicide: both are dreaded and forbidden.
—IRVING STENGEL, *Suicide and Attempted Suicide*

So much has been written about suicide and so little about what happens to the survivor. This chapter begins our narrative about what happens to all survivors.

If death has a sting, death by suicide has many. The first: the shock of learning about the death itself.

A SON:

I was in bed. About two A.M. I remember my mother coming upstairs. She told each of us in turn. She was weeping, of course. My immediate reaction was shock; I cried for an hour or two. My mother told us right away that he hooked up a hose to the exhaust pipe. I remember her trying to explain it in a sugar-coated sense: "Your father had problems, he couldn't cope." But at that age I don't think I fully comprehended.

A FATHER:

I drove home on the particular day in question. I noticed there was a car in the garage and there was some activity, but

I simply thought my son had brought the car home and was working on it. When I walked into the house, someone came to me and said my son had killed himself.

ANOTHER SON:

When I came home from school my father sat me down with my other brothers and sisters. They had been pulled out of school ahead of time and informed that my mother was dead. He sat us down at the kitchen table and said that he was going to give us news that was the hardest thing a father could ever tell his kids. Then he told us that our mother was dead. There was a long pause. Then my little sisters asked, "How? Why?" They didn't really understand what was going on. I think at the time I was definitely old enough to understand the concept of death, although I just kept on trying to figure out how things were going to change, what it was going to be like, whether I would miss her. I didn't talk about it much, just thought a lot about it, wondering what was going to happen, why it happened. I never asked about anything.

For many, if not most, survivors, the anxiety and the terror do not begin on the day that someone dies; long before, sometimes three, four, or five years earlier, their loved one has attempted suicide. For years, then, they have been living with the knowledge that the attempt might come again, that this time it might be successful. For Ruth, the mother of Beth, and for Beth's fiancé, Evan, who had known her for eight years, it was a continual watch. Finally, the watch came to an end.

RUTH:

She had been living in the city, starting a new teaching job that she was very apprehensive about. Elementary school. She was twenty-four years old. As the days came closer to the start of school, she became anxious, and we were all aware of it. She was very good about sharing her emotions. Ever since her attempts to commit suicide, we were all on the "watch out." Evan had been living with her just prior to the beginning of school, and he had just left ten days before. So she was alone in her apartment in the city. She called two days before to say that she was not going to go to teach the next day. My husband was home.

He invited, he insisted, that she come home right away. So when I got home that evening, I started talking with her, and she expressed her anxiety. She didn't say anything about wanting to die, but she did say she wasn't well prepared, she didn't know what to do, she'd already told them she was taking the next day off, she couldn't handle it anymore. She was home the next day, she didn't go to school. We spent the whole day discussing various options. My husband said, quit right away, just quit, relieve all pressures. She said that's very nice of him to say quit, but "I'm not sure that's really what I want."

She made a date to see a psychiatrist, but decided at one point there was no sense in seeing her; there was nothing that she could do. I insisted, so she went, and she came back and said she loved the psychiatrist. "She's really good. She feels I should go back tomorrow." She spoke with Evan, who was always willing to talk with her.

A slight foreign accent tinges Ruth's storytelling, but she has a good command of English, and she knows what she wants to say. Evan, on the other hand, is soft-spoken, hesitant. One has the sense he is on the verge of tears.

EVAN:

I remember that day very well, because we spoke two or three times. I was on the phone for about forty-five minutes. In the nine o'clock call she had been saying all day that she was depressed and thinking of killing herself. "No matter what happens, take care of my dog." "What does that mean?" "I don't know." And I said, "Are you planning to kill yourself?" and she said, "I don't know."

RUTH:

There was lots of talking, right from the beginning. Including my husband. Beth was always ready to talk about how she felt.

EVAN:

An indication of how much we did talk was that she could tell me that she wanted to kill herself and I could not be shocked by it. I had had dozens of conversations with her about her death, so it got to the point where she could tell me that and whatever I did or didn't do, I did or didn't do. It was an indication of how much we were all involved in the way she framed the world, and how regular that kind of discussion had become.

Next morning Beth's father called, and he's called only three times in the eight years I've known this family. He said, "It doesn't look good. You'd better get down here right away." I remember very well how I felt. I was driving down here, and the whole car ride I was crying and saying, "Please God, don't let her be dead," and I don't even believe in God. And then I got here and I saw all the cars in the driveway and I figured the worst had happened.

It was Ruth who discovered Beth, dead next to an empty bottle of sleeping pills. Somehow, they had never expected her to kill herself at home.

Discovering the body can be a shattering experience, even for adults. It is worse for a child. It stays with a person an entire lifetime.

MAY:
I was eight, so it must have been 1931. On Christmas Day my father killed himself at home—he hanged himself and, unfortunately, I was the one who found him, which was very difficult, and it still bothers me. Every once in a while my eyes fill up when I think about it. It's always with me. I was his favorite child and I'd been reading to him and he told me he was tired, to go away; he was going to sleep and I should come back later.

I can remember a lot of details about the whole thing. When I found him, I ran over and grabbed his legs. I knew somehow to try to hold him. But it was too late.

I was his favorite—why should he have left me? I think about it a lot. The other day, there was an ad in a magazine and the way they had photographed this woman's feet it looked as if she was hanging, and it shocked me.

I obviously will never get over it.

Sarah is twenty-three years old, very much an older sister—wary, but willing both to listen and to talk. Patricia, seated across the table

16

from her, is twenty and shy. She has trouble finding words, until she begins to tell the story of the suicide itself. Then her vocabulary gets significantly better. They live in a small house in a working-class neighborhood. It was Sarah who woke up one morning to discover that her mother had killed herself.

> I don't know who discovered the body. I guess I did ... didn't I?
> I kind of had a feeling. I was bringing the garbage pail out and I saw the fog on the window of the garage, and I knew someone had to be in there. Or an animal. Then I heard the car running, and I had this feeling, and I was afraid to open it, and I ran and woke Patricia up.

Patricia takes up the story. As with many survivors, the details of the event itself remain blurred, even two years afterward.

> I still to this day don't know who opened the garage door. I don't even know how I got out of my door—from the bed to the garage. Her radio was on upstairs, so I still wasn't sure. I was afraid to look.

The two sisters (then only eighteen and twenty-one) did look. Nothing in their previous experience had prepared them for what they had to do: turn off the motor of the family car in which their mother lay dead from carbon monoxide poisoning. They called the ambulance and the police.

PATRICIA:
> We know a lot of the cops in the area, so they were a little more sympathetic, but they did have to take pictures and ask who found her and that sort of thing. This cop was nervous; he was basically just sitting here. He didn't know what to do or say.

In other cases, police have not just sat there. Many survivors report that detectives spend a good deal of time looking for evidence of "foul play"; they do not—or cannot—accept, at face value, the story of a suicide. One woman told me that her daughter's apartment had been

17

sealed for a month while police investigated the possibility of murder. The way survivors are questioned is often vigorous and accusatory as the police go about their business.

One of the reasons the statistics on suicide are so misleading is that in many deaths—by shotgun, automobile, drugs—it is not always clear whether the dead person intended suicide or not. Coroners and police, the family and friends, often decide it is easier to fend off stigma and other repercussions by calling the death an accident. This has ramifications not only for insurance companies but for the entire train of events that follow. Family members have to decide whether to live with this bending of reality forever or to change their story later.

Sometimes death isn't immediate, and the survivor has to contend with rushing a relative to the hospital and waiting to find out what will happen. Martha was at work when her sister called from Florida to say that their mother had tried to kill herself by drinking from a bottle of corrosive liquid cleanser.

> I remember being shocked and on the verge of hysteria, thinking that I had to get down there and I had to get in touch with my husband, and I was ready to kill the page operator. She just kept saying, "Page is busy." And then finally one of the secretaries got through to my husband. I don't even remember the flight down, I think I was just so in a state of shock. I just couldn't believe it; I was afraid that she was going to be dead by the time I got there and I wouldn't be able to see or talk to her.

For some, the shock is double; one, the death of a parent or other loved one; two, when they discover—inadvertently, perhaps—that the death was by suicide.

The reaction of people outside the family now becomes important as survivors struggle to return to some kind of equilibrium in their lives. Friends and neighbors, employers and employees, become factors in the way we begin to feel about ourselves and the death.

Some survivors comment:

> A suicide survivor shouldn't feel ashamed . . . but we are made to feel that way.

Your friends avoid you. No one calls. You're alone.

I just want to run away. People say, "What did you *do* to her?"

The public attitude is that people who kill themselves are crazy. That attitude attaches to us, the family. We're made to feel as if we, too, are sick.

My in-laws acted as though I were responsible for it all.

People come up to you and say, "Did you see it? Did your family see it? What was wrong?" You feel like you're being interrogated. And all you know is that someone you loved died.

I feel I have a big sign on me—"My son committed suicide."

Suicide is a public admission that my love for my child wasn't enough.

These statements come from a wide variety of survivors: working-class people and the rich; suburbanites and city dwellers; young and old. The milieu seems to make no difference. Socially, suicide is considered to be an aberrant act, and the family of the person who kills himself comes in for some powerful public opprobrium. Of course, these attitudes have a historical base. It is only recently, for instance, that organized religions have changed from a punitive approach toward the suicidal person to a relatively beneficent one. For centuries, people who killed themselves were buried at crossroads, their hearts often pierced with a stake. Survivors were shunned, excommunicated, robbed of the suicide's possessions. (People who attempted suicide received only slightly less disapprobation: They were often whipped or sentenced to prison.) The present century has seen amelioration of official attitudes by both religion and society—we no longer send people who attempt suicide to prison—but there are still clergy who look on the death of a person by suicide as a sinful act. This is a double-edged sword. Some priests and rabbis believe that labeling suicide a sin results in a smaller number of suicides within those religions that decry it, but it is also true that calling it a sin brings down

19

society's wrath on the "sinner's" family—the survivors. Society hangs on to many of the old ways of looking at suicide: It is still a shameful act, smacking of insanity or satanic intervention. It is still difficult to hold a conversation about someone's suicide without running into punitive attitudes.

So the attitude toward survivors is often equally condemnatory. Patricia and Sarah told us that someone in the town blamed *them* for their mother's death. Someone else blamed their father because he had been separated from their mother for eight years. Other survivors had similar stories:

SEAN:
One friend's father would take us bowling, but that lasted only for so long. My mother's dentist suggested we should leave town because my father committed suicide.

RUTH:
Our family doctor told us we were to blame because Beth hadn't been given drugs. Beth wouldn't *take* drugs. And this was a close friend, too!

WANDA:
That was the most amazing thing—to see how people reacted. I had two close friends, a couple, who didn't call me. Not for months. I was so shocked.

But there is supportive reaction, too. Sometimes it comes from the family and sometimes from the outside.

EVAN:
And then friends came. We didn't sit shiva [a seven-day official period of mourning in the Jewish religion; friends and relatives are constantly in attendance] officially, but there were so many people here, it almost felt like a party. And there was a lot of support.

During this period, when people are sitting around depressed, crying, angry, fearful, when children who have been free from nightmares for years begin having them again, it is difficult to know to whom to turn. Despite the often disapproving attitude of the official churches, several survivors talked to us of the help given them by individual clergy. This was especially important when the decision about a funeral or memorial service had to be faced. Shall we discuss the suicide? Ignore it? What should we say? (Unfortunately, many clerics don't seem to know what to say, either. Perhaps embarrassed by the event, many try to say what cannot be said or try to cover up because the family wants the truth denied. Some survivor groups have written pamphlets for funeral directors and clergy to give them some idea of what it's like for the survivor after a suicide, some suggestions as to how to behave, and some hints about what to say—what helps and what doesn't.)

EVAN:
I think a person who was very important was the rabbi who came. I have very little respect for clerics, but he came that day and in a certain way he took control. He sat us down. He let us know what was going to happen. I found it very helpful to have him here.

RUTH:
He asked us all about Beth and let us talk about her. Then the eulogy was absolutely remarkable. What he did was, rather than condemn her choice, he made us all understand it without legitimizing it. He drew on metaphors from her life. I don't know what inspired him, but it was beautiful.

What—and how much—should a survivor say to other people? Some families can tell their relatives the truth, but what about their employer or employees? Each survivor picks his own approach, but almost all are fraught with perceived dangers. One person told us he was afraid to tell his employer the truth for fear he wouldn't be trusted on the job again. "I thought they would think I was crazy, like my brother." Another was worried because she kept breaking out in tears on the job and didn't know how to tell her boss what was going on. Still another was furious because her employer had no sympathy for her, even after she told him that her son had killed himself ("I don't

21

know whether my boss was uptight about suicide or just wasn't a sympathetic person, but he kept telling me to get my act together"). Another simply said, "You go to a job . . . if you're lucky enough to have one. Sitting at home is worse!"

Wanda felt she was especially lucky.

> My workplace was terrific. People were nice. My supervisor—when she spoke with me . . . I just went in there and cried. The director of the department called me into his office one day just to talk. The assistant director called me in to talk. People were great.

If you don't know what to tell someone you work for, what about the press? Patricia was particularly upset about the way newspapers and television played up suicide. It was a year when there had been a large number of teenage suicides in the county.

> PATRICIA:
> I don't think it helps at all, talking about it on the news. What are you telling people? People who don't know you say they do know you; people ask if she was depressed. It just gives people ideas, to be honest. That year when my mother did it, suicide was so publicized. I began to wonder, did she think, "Well, if they can do it, why haven't I been able to do it up to this point?" I really feel that way, because her problems had been going on for ten or twelve years, and in that year when everything had been in the news, she did it one month later.

The notion that publicizing something leads others to emulate it is neither new nor limited to suicide. It has been suggested about sex, drugs, murder, and racism. It is, however, an especially recurrent theme among suicide survivors. At the Rutgers conference many of the survivors were insistent that it had been loose references to suicide in the press or in popular songs and the romanticizing of suicide in soap operas that had led their sons and daughters to kill themselves.

The question of how the media report any violent act has long been debated. Is it a good or bad thing that we learn about the details of a suicide on the air or in our morning papers? Does it make a difference? Patricia would have the newspapers report the event, but not the details. Others we spoke to very much wanted the details of suicide described, believing that if you or I read about the horrors of the event, we might be deterred from taking our own lives. It is an age-old argument, not likely to be settled by random opinion-taking.

Interestingly enough, though there is much evidence that the number of suicides has increased in recent years, the fact is that there is less detail and less volume of reporting about suicide in newspapers than there was one hundred years ago when the incidence of suicide appears to have been smaller. A few examples:

> New York, June 3, 1882.
> Denton Miller, a clerk for Wheeler, Parsons, and Hays, jewelers of #2 Maiden Lane, shot himself yesterday in the Western Hotel. He was the son of Arthur Miller and lived with his parents at #64 Monroe Street, Brooklyn. Mr. Miller said yesterday his son was 34. He was married to Miss Cholmwell of Norwalk and two years later divorced. Denton had been despondent for a long while but had seemed quite cheerful on Tuesday when he went fishing.

The article about Denton Miller, appearing in *The New York Times,* was four column inches long (that is, one column wide, four inches in length) in a newspaper that had only eight pages that day. In other words, though Mr. Miller was apparently an unknown, his suicide was something to which the *Times* devoted considerable space. To be sure, this was an era during which all newspapers gave ample coverage to crimes in their "police blotters," but the fact remains that suicide was given significant newspaper space. After discussing the bare facts about Denton Miller's death, the article reports on interviews with both his father and his brother. It describes in some detail the way Denton died ("an ugly wound") and the fact that he had left his brother a note. Further . . .

> Mr. Miller said he was unable to think of any reason for the suicide. "My son was in no financial trouble nor any trouble with a woman."

The article is straightforward, lengthy, and earnest in its effort to discuss the suicide. The newspaper has no hesitation in naming names, giving addresses, and probing for reasons. The practice of writing and publishing lengthy and revealing stories about deaths by suicide continued in the *Times* for thirty or forty years. What's striking about the stories is not only their length, but the fact that they made no effort to hide the identity of family or to cast shame on the act itself. This contrasts dramatically with present practice. While many more suicides are actually reported in today's *Times* (a newspaper often comprising one hundred pages in its daily edition), the weight given to such stories during the police-blotter days was greater and the kind of coverage quite different. Most such items today are no more than one to two column inches. Missing are interviews with the family; missing, too, are details of name and place. More interesting, there seems to be less analysis as to cause of the suicide than there was in earlier years. Some examples:

February 19, 1954. Page 29. [1 column inch]
Miss J. Ford, a 26-year-old secretary to the Consul General of Pakistan in New York, was found dead last night in the gas-filled kitchenette of her one-room apartment at 140 E. 52nd St. Pending an autopsy report, the death is listed as suicide.

July 1, 1954. [1 1/2 column inches]
A Brooklyn boy who failed a French course and an entrance examination to Brooklyn Technical High School hanged himself after school yesterday by his dog's leash. . . . He suspended himself from a shower rod.

June 2, 1983. [1 inch]
A 23-year-old New Jersey man leaped to his death from the observation deck of the Empire State building yesterday morning. The police said the man, J. Larkin of Mount Holly, climbed the protective fence on the 88th floor shortly after 1:00 P.M. and was killed instantly when he struck the pavement on East 33rd St.

A cursory interpretation of these comparisons would seem to be that perceptions are wrong on several counts: Today's newspaper coverage of suicide is much less conspicuous than a hundred years ago; the diminished coverage does not seem to curtail the increase in suicides; but neither does the present coverage seem to have much to do with present upward rates of suicide in adults. In adolescents, however, it is a different matter. Research points to a "cluster" effect—when publicity is given to a suicide by adolescents, other young people seem to take this as an invitation to kill themselves. This poses a problem for the media that goes beyond the scope of this book: whether to maintain the unhealthy silence that surrounds suicide or risk engendering more adolescent suicides by reporting on previous ones.

Time passes for the survivor. The funeral or memorial service has come and gone. Family members have gone back to work. Perhaps a month has passed, and survivors begin to expect that they will be able to go about their business without the emotional chaos of the past weeks.

In general, this expectation is unreal. The effect of the suicide does not dissipate in that fashion. And the question that came first to many survivors may very well be the one that lasts the longest: "Why?" The problem, of course, is that most of us don't get a chance to discuss that question with the one person who is closest to having the answer. Being left behind as a result of someone's suicide has been likened to having an argument with someone who has the last word. You don't even have the opportunity to say good-bye.

One phenomenon of this period strikes many survivors as disturbing and bewildering. In fact, it's a common event, experienced not only by suicide survivors but by those whose relatives have died a natural death. It's the fantasy that your loved one is still around.

Anne-Marie is a woman in her thirties whose brother has only recently killed himself. Her life was already overshadowed by a mother who was schizophrenic and institutionalized and a father she never knew. She has been talking about how lonely she feels, how the suicide broke up what was left of the family's togetherness. Suddenly she stops and thinks of something else.

. . . I don't know, crazy things happen, like a few days later I walked into the bank, and I saw this little bird around the chande-

25

lier. I was actually convinced it was my brother, coming back to say, "Go on, Anne-Marie, it'll be okay." I'd see the bird flying around, and it was him, coming back to talk to me.

This particular discussion was going on in a self-help group where there was a wide range of experience. A woman in the corner who had said almost nothing up to this point now spoke up. Her daughter had killed herself five years earlier, longer ago than anyone else in the group.

... I used to see the little birds, or I'd feel someone tugging, and I thought I was crazy. Most everybody I know has some kind of experience like that. Wishful thinking. The blond head in front of me, by some miracle, was going to be my daughter.

'Course I don't think that anymore.

It is at this point that survivors may begin to feel the need for what has been termed *postvention,* help from the helping professions. They may begin to ask why so many people around them seem either oblivious to their pain or are cruel in the way they are reacting to it; why the support that might be available to them if their loved ones had died in a car accident is absent because the death was a suicide; why they are so unprepared for this crisis in their lives.

Chapter 2

EMOTIONAL REACTIONS
TO SUICIDE

Suicide is more painful for the family than other kinds of death, and harder to acknowledge. The survivor often suffers from guilt and shame that prevent normal mourning.
      —The Harvard Medical School Mental Health Letter

Suicide survivors suffer in three ways: first, because they are grieving for a dead person; second, because they are suffering from a traumatic experience—in fact, they are victims of what is called Posttraumatic Stress Disorder; third, because people don't talk about suicide, and the silence that surrounds it gets in the way of the healing that comes with normal mourning.

In chapter 11, we talk at length about silence. In this chapter we deal mainly with grief and trauma.

TRAUMA

Psychological trauma is the result of a severely damaging experience, such as the death of a child, becoming orphaned, being in a bad car accident, being raped or beaten, and other sudden, violent events.

When people have been hit hard psychologically, it has to hurt.

Beyond hurting, being hit hard has ongoing psychological consequences.

There is a well-known disorder that characterizes traumatized people. In World War I it was called shell shock. Later, in World War II,
it came to be called battle neurosis. Following the Vietnam War, many
veterans were recognized to be suffering from what is now called
Posttraumatic Stress Disorder after they returned to the States. In fact,
such behavior is common to psychological trauma, both in and out of
war.

Sufferers of the disorder are not crazy. But they are disturbed. They
are reacting to the traumatic experience they have had. They feel
pain, disorientation, and other things that are so different from the
way they ordinarily feel that their lives seem turned upside down.

For the survivor, suicide is a trauma. Survivors need to know that
what they are suffering is not only the grief that follows the death of
a loved one but this well-known psychological phenomenon, shared
by millions of other people who have had severely disturbing experiences.

There is a manual that mental health workers use called the *Diag-
nostic and Statistical Manual of the American Psychiatric Association.*
In the current version of that book, symptoms of Posttraumatic Stress
Disorder are described. Here is a paraphrase. It is likely that any
survivor of a suicide will recognize the symptoms immediately.

People suffering from this disorder:

Reexperience the trauma in one of the following ways:
- They have recurrent recollections of the event.
- They have dreams of the event.
- They suddenly feel as if the event were recurring.

Experience a numbing or reduced involvement with the world by:
- A lessening of interest in important activities
- A feeling of detachment from others
- A flat, emotionless feeling

Have some of the following symptoms:
- Sleep disturbances
- Guilt about surviving

28

- Trouble concentrating, loss of memory
- Exaggerated startle response
- They avoid some of the activities that arouse recollection of the trauma.

The symptoms of Posttraumatic Stress Disorder can show up immediately or not for months or years. They can last a short while; they can last a lifetime. Because humans are very good at hiding feelings from themselves, especially when they're very painful, survivors may experience nightmares that seem unrelated to the death of their loved one. These may occur soon after the suicide or much later—sometimes years later. Hidden as the message of these nightmares may be, they are often an indication that the fears, angers, and guilts of the survivor are still very much with him.

Suicide survivors should know, and will surely understand, that the symptoms are more severe when people are reacting not to natural disasters but to "man-made" ones (wars, assaults, imprisonment, torture, or the murder or suicide of a loved one).

Suicide survivors should know, and we hope this book will help them understand, that both the severity and the duration of the symptoms depend on how people who have been traumatized are subsequently treated.

Having to go it alone makes recovery harder. Having no chance to talk about the experience makes it harder. Having no chance to understand what has happened and why it happened—guilt, stigma, and silence—all make recovery harder.

REACTIONS TO SUICIDE

So far we have talked about Posttraumatic Stress Disorder in general. What about reactions to suicide? These seem to have some special dimensions. Following a suicide, there is both the suffering from grief and the reaction to a traumatic event.

SARAH, whose mother killed herself:
For a long time I had dreams—and I still do—nightmares.

29

Like she would try to kill me. If she hadn't killed herself, I don't think I would have felt that way—about a natural death or something. With a suicide, you have to deal with the loss, with the guilt, and with the questioning, all at once. It's very different.

ARTHUR, a father:
It's a different kind of death from others. I wish I could say it was an accident. It would make it so much easier.

But it wasn't an accident. It was a suicide, and here is how many survivors react to it.

The First Wave

(There is no fixed order to these "waves" of emotions, but the reactions often do come in this fashion.)

"I didn't know where to turn."
"I didn't know what was happening to me."
"I didn't believe it."
"I *refused* to believe it."
"Thank God it wasn't me!"
"How could he leave me like this?"

"Looking back on what we did, it was an emotional roller coaster, where she would be down and I was finally getting to the point where I was up; and then I got depressed, and she was up."

"It was hell."

"It was more difficult than the natural death of a parent. It's the most terrible thing anyone can go through in their entire life."

Often, at first, the survivor is stunned by what has befallen him. He attempts to deny it, even to the extent of saying it wasn't a suicide, that something else must have happened. He feels helpless: How can he get on with his life? How can he go to work? How will he get on without

30

the loved one? The suddenness of the event, and his unpreparedness, leave him without any of the prior working-through of grief that often goes with normal death. For instance, often there has been no long illness, no medicines, no visiting doctors, no bed rest, nothing to prepare the survivor for death, to allow him to say good-bye. Even when suicide follows upon previous attempts, the survivor is unprepared. "I just didn't think she would do it" is a constant refrain.

For a small group of survivors, there is sudden relief—relief that the chain of attempts is over, that their loved one's pain is finished, that their struggle with the loved one is also over. But this relief often gives way to guilt as the survivor blames himself for feeling relieved, or for just being a survivor.

For most survivors, after shock and helplessness, the strongest feeling is the recognition that they have been rejected in a profound and personal way. The suicide survivor knows that he has been left behind by someone who chose to do it.

Finally, there is blame, some immediate effort to get away from the guilty feelings—to find someone else who is responsible.

A FATHER:
Everyone was sitting around, blaming, blaming, blaming. No one was doing anything useful.

A SISTER:
In terms of coping, I did every single thing wrong. When I heard about my brother at two in the morning, I told my children that it was an accident. When I went to tell my father, we went to his sister's house and we spent the day finding out who was to blame. My father thought my mother's family was crazy. She wasn't there to defend them, so someone else in the family thought of someone on *his* side of the family who was just as crazy, and then everyone decided to blame my sister. We didn't talk about it, there was no funeral, there was no ritual. The family—wife and three children—moved very quickly out of their house and I lost contact with them for a number of years.

To sum up: The first wave seems to be taken up with shock, denial, helplessness, relief (sometimes), and blame.

31

The Second Wave

Anger

A DAUGHTER:

I remember driving up to work and waves of emotion coming over me. I'd be either extremely angry or I'd be screaming in pain in the car—thankful the windows were shut. These waves of feeling came over me and I just gave in to them; feeling that I would never get over it.

A HUSBAND:

I feel very angry about this whole thing. She walked out on me and left me.

ANNE-MARIE, whose brother killed himself:

I scream, I yell out the window. I say, "How could you do this to me?" I throw things. I have *hatred* toward my sister-in-law, intense hatred. I have never felt this angry in my whole entire life. Angrier than I ever was at my mother or my father for not being there. It's so frustrating! Because I always had, at least, my brother. I keep thinking, "Why did you do this to me? Why did you do this to me?"

A WIFE:

I feel like I'm a widow and I'm divorced. I feel like the S.O.B. left me.

A MOTHER:

You give a child life, then he destroys it.

A NIECE:

I loved my uncle, but I can't forgive him for what he did to his children and his family. I'm angry because I can't ever feel the same as I did before about him. I can't keep the happy memories because of the anger at what he did.

The anger that survivors feel toward the dead person is often not expressed out loud, nor is it even experienced as anger because the survivor feels too guilty.

AMANDA, a woman whose daughter was an addict:

It's hard to be angry at somebody whose life was so tormented and tortured and had such a miserable, rotten time. I was angry at her when she was alive, believe me, taking those pills, but I cannot feel angry at her now. I have a lot of anger in me, but I can never direct it at her.

It *is* hard to be angry at the people we love, especially when it's the kind of anger that is deep and continuous, the kind of anger that lasts. And yet we all experience some of that anger at the people we live with: We're ambivalent some of the time. We can't help it, that's part of the human experience. Being ambivalent is part of being human.

So when someone dies a violent, self-inflicted death while we are still in the midst of our ambivalence, or worse yet, actually feeling angry, we feel bad about ourselves. If we now get angry over their death, it makes matters worse. After all, it's not reasonable to be angry at a victim. One of the survivor's responses to the anger he feels at his loved one's suicide, then, is guilt—guilt over the anger that he, a survivor, feels toward a dead person.

Guilt

If there is one pervasive reaction that survivors have to suicide, it is guilt. Suddenly, there seem to be endless reasons to feel responsible for the death. What could I have done to keep the loved one alive? Did I do enough? Was I neglectful? Did I ignore warning signs?

"I should have known he was going to do it."

"I should have known he was a manic-depressive. We could have put him in the hospital."

"Why couldn't I have been a better person?"

"Why didn't I see the warning signs?"

"If only I'd been more thoughtful . . . if only I'd cared more . . . if only I'd been a better person . . . if, if, if."

However it's phrased, whether it comes from an adult or a child, the pervading thought is that if we'd done more, loved them more, or been around more, things might have turned out differently: Our loved ones would still be alive. Survivors have a sense of guilt that suggests, "Somehow, we should have prevented the suicide."

For children, there's a kind of magical thinking: "I was angry at my father, he got sick and died. Therefore, I caused it." But adults, too, think that way. Or believe that something they did—or didn't do—caused the suicide.

MARIA, whose twenty-one-year-old nephew shot himself:
It's just been a nightmare. This has ended my brother's marriage. My parents are devastated. It's just so hard, because we don't know why, and I keep thinking, *What did we do?*

Angela is one of the two people who started a self-help group. She and Frances had a close friend who killed herself. The three of them shared a beach house.

ANGELA:
The day before she died, she talked to me about committing suicide. She was a very dedicated Roman Catholic and was quite concerned: She said the Catholic Church has frowned on suicide in the past. "Do you think anyone goes to hell for committing suicide?" she asked me. And I said no, I don't think anyone goes to hell for that. Eighteen hours later she did it.

I don't know that my guilt in that will ever go away completely.

JEANETTE:
For months I was convinced that I was responsible. It was as if *I* had pulled the trigger, not him. It was crazy. I wasn't near the house, but I felt that I was to blame.

Larry hadn't thought about the suicide in his life for many years—until recently. Bearded, withdrawn, he spoke as if he didn't have the right to express his feelings.

34

Nineteen years ago, about this time of year, my roommate committed suicide. He got poor grades, went into the Marine Reserves for six months, then got out and went into another school, where he got good grades. He thought that the Marines would make a man out of him. I kept saying, "I don't see anything wrong with you."

He went to Las Vegas, lost some money, drove back, and blew up the engine in his parent's car. Went to two ex-girlfriends and, in the same day, asked them both to marry him, and they both said no. He and his mother suffered from migraine headaches and he overdosed on his headache pills.

I belong to a suicide prevention organization, and recently all the old feelings came up, many of them involving guilt. I wasn't very studious, and I kept thinking, if I'd been a different kind of person, he'd have gotten better grades. He asked me to write a term paper, but I didn't have the time, and he flunked the course. I focus on these small things, which I realize are ridiculous, but I ruminate on them.

RALPH, whose brother killed himself, talks about his sister-in-law's reaction to the suicide:

For a year or so she would call, at first every couple of weeks or so, and go over the whole thing. "If I only hadn't gone to the airport—if I hadn't stayed up all night fixing that dress for my daughter—it wouldn't have happened." I kept trying to say that it would happen sometime, that there was nothing she could do. But she wouldn't listen.

Ralph's wife, MAY, whose brother also killed himself:*

I feel some guilt, too, and it's kind of a crazy sort of thing. I had been told that I had multiple sclerosis and I told my brother about it and of course the whole family knew, and shortly after that I was going to be in New York at a meeting and my brother

*Both Ralph's and May's fathers killed themselves; each had a brother who committed suicide. A family in which there are multiple suicides is not unusual. In fact, one suicide often does seem to engender another, a tragedy which we discuss at length in chapter 10.

wanted to come to see us and I said, "Don't make the trip; we'll be very busy and we're going to be moving back to New York in the spring anyway, so wait and I'll see you then." And he killed himself before I had a chance to see him, and I keep thinking . . .

While many factors contribute to the guilt that survivors feel—a survivor had a strained relationship with the dead person, or the loved one attempted suicide many times and the survivor could not get him to accept help, and so on—one of the most powerful and poisonous contributors to guilt is what could be called the accusation from the grave. The dead person often appears to be pointing a finger at the survivor: "You failed me." "You did this to me, you did that to me. You made me do it!"

This sense of a pointing finger can be there in the very suicide itself; it can be embedded in the unfinished conversations, the unspoken anger, the ambivalence.

Both Sarah and Patricia seem to feel that accusation from their dead mother, who had made suicide attempts before.

SARAH:

It was strange because we had had an argument, and for a long time afterward, I felt the argument was responsible for her death. Not that she hadn't tried suicide before. Overall, I knew it wasn't my fault, but the timing I felt responsible for.

It was weird, because I never left her in an argument feeling mad. But I came home that day and I said, "I can't talk to her." It was one of those times when I'd had it. Usually she'd give clues, like "Life isn't worth living." That night, Patricia said, "Do you think she's going to do anything?" And I said, "No, she's not in that frame of mind."

PATRICIA:

Sarah said, "Why don't you go up and talk to her?" And I said, "No, I'll go up in the morning." Very strange, because I usually went up. . . .

SARAH:

Me, too.

PATRICIA:

... I used to go up there and try to straighten everything out so we'd know that ... so we could pick up tomorrow and everything would be normal again.

SARAH:

I never left a time where we didn't talk about it.

PATRICIA:

I felt, afterward, maybe if I had gone upstairs and ironed this out, it wouldn't have led to this.

It seems as if something was operating that night that was different from all the other nights, all the other arguments. Perhaps their mother was trying to keep them from settling the argument so that they would feel guilty after her death. Perhaps she was simply trying to separate herself from them. By keeping the argument going, it might have been easier for her to say, "The hell with you; I'll go kill myself." Or perhaps she didn't want to settle the argument, because then she wouldn't be hurt enough or angry enough or in despair enough to go through with the suicide.

These are, of course, only speculations. What does seem clear, however, is that both Sarah and Patricia felt, and continue to feel, the accusation from the grave. And so do many other survivors.

Part of what is so painful about the guilt that survivors feel is that there is no way they can find out from the dead person whether the guilt is justified. They cannot ask if it *was* their behavior that was the final blow. They can only speculate—and continue to feel guilty.

Shame

Despite the fact that there has been some movement away from official stigmatizing of suicide, survivors often feel the shame that comes from neighbors, former friends, and other segments of society. One researcher tells these stories:

One woman thought, as long as six years after her husband's suicide, that if people found out about it, they would think that insanity ran in the family. She left her home right after the death because of the negative feelings she got from her neighbors.

The fiancée of a twenty-three-year-old man killed herself. He felt that his friends didn't understand his feelings, that people viewed him negatively because of his fiancée's death. He moved away.

The suicide of a mother left a fifteen-year-old girl ashamed. It had been a front-page story, and during the investigation she was bothered by the fact that the police did not even talk to her. Her impression was "They didn't give a damn." Her father told her to lie to friends about her mother's death. A year and a half later she felt absolutely abandoned by both her family and her friends. She had no normal social life.

Anxiety

"I was afraid it would happen to my other children."
"I was afraid to go out."
"I was afraid to stay at home by myself."
"I'll never be loved again."

The survivor's life has been shaken and, not surprisingly, survivors are vulnerable. They can't trust their world and the people in it ever to treat them fairly again.

A MOTHER:

Now when I come home, I'm afraid another tragedy will have occurred. Suicide is an option now.

A FATHER:

It was almost a year and a half before one of our kids could leave home for the evening without one of us becoming panicked.

A SEVENTEEN-YEAR-OLD SON:

It's been a year now, but I'm still afraid to go out with a girl. It's like every female is going to walk out on me. I get this cold-sweat feeling in my stomach, and I can't even ask someone out. I just *know* something's going to happen.

38

To sum up: The second wave hits the survivor with anger, guilt, shame, and anxiety.

The Third Wave

When people lose someone (or something) important to them, they feel sad. And they feel angry at the loss.

When people are angry, but feel guilty or frightened and powerless, they often turn the anger in on themselves. The result is depression.

Suicide survivors have reason to be sad and reason to be depressed. But depression, in the case of suicide survivors, is often long lasting and deep. It paralyzes people. They lose weight or overeat; they can't form new relationships because their self-esteem is so low: if one person rejects them, so will everyone else. Some can't get jobs, some are too depressed to ask for a raise. Suicide committed by someone they love leaves them in the depths of despair.

MARK, whose girlfriend killed herself a year ago:

Before, I had the feeling I could control what happened to me. After Angela died, it was strange, because I never felt in control again. I wanted to go back—before she died—and have something to say about what happened to her. But, of course, I couldn't. It couldn't be undone. And now I don't feel like I have control over anything in my life.

AMANDA:

. . . then I broke up with my husband, and I moved, and I started to fall apart. I'm disconnected. I've had unnecessary operations. I have no family. No one really cares about me.

THOMAS:

I sit around the house all day. Sometimes I sleep for twelve hours at a time. I don't call anyone, and nobody calls me. Or if they do, I find I don't have anything to say to them. I feel this incredible heavy fog; it sits on me, keeping me down. People tell me my voice is so low, so soft, that they can't understand me. But I don't care. It's all just too much.

39

To sum up the third wave: The survivors often experience depression and low self-esteem.

The Fourth Wave

It's an amazing fact, but it seems that within the first six months following a suicide, almost every survivor goes to his family physician for aid. One researcher lists some of the symptoms:

> Crying spells, inability to sleep, fear of being alone, migraines, ulcers, heart attacks, exhaustion. The survivors are on medication—mostly liquor for men, mostly tranquilizers for women.

Others point to equally serious psychological problems, from a sense of emptiness, to the inability to form new relationships, to phobias, to anxieties about the most common daily events.

One of the saddest things about these psychological and psychosomatic responses to suicide is that many survivors don't connect them. They may, in fact, often not talk about the suicide to their physicians. In addition, they may actually feel guilty about their symptoms and may not seek help from physicians or mental health professionals. Posttraumatic Stress Disorder, says one physician, just isn't well enough known by either its victims or by society in general.

> The reluctance of [survivors] to seek help stems from such factors as their inability to understand their symptoms (nightmares, inability to sleep, anxiety), the inability of those close to them to believe and support them, and the lack of knowledge of sources of assistance in the community.
>
> Because the public has not been educated about posttraumatic stress disorder, these individuals often live with a sense of isolation and guilt about their crippling symptoms. They are reluctant to seek help.

One of the psychological reactions to suicide by the survivor is, sadly, ironically, that they wish to kill themselves.

This is so prevalent that survivor groups use the word *normal* to refer to these suicidal thoughts. Almost every survivor seems to have thought of suicide at one point or another.

But sometimes the survivor actually attempts suicide.

And sometimes he is successful. *Omega,* a journal devoted to aspects of death and dying, reports in one study that out of seventeen children of parents who committed suicide, five attempted suicide and two completed it.

The American Association of Suicidology, which delves into all areas of suicide, states that survivors are much more likely to kill themselves than are the rest of the population.

To sum up the fourth wave: Survivors suffer a wide range of psychological and psychosomatic (physical) problems, including a propensity toward suicide itself.

Denial

Mention needs to be made of one more emotional reaction that doesn't fall conveniently into any of the "waves." Sometimes a survivor simply cannot take in the enormity of the event that has befallen him or her. The denial that ensues is in some cases a refusal to accept the event itself; the death is explained away in some other fashion. In others, it is a refusal to deal with the emotional consequences of the event.

For example, Frank and his wife had been separated for eight years. She was an alcoholic and eventually shut herself in the garage and asphyxiated herself. (Their two daughters, Sarah and Patricia, have already figured in this chapter.) When we went to see the two young women, their father was in the house, apparently not interested in being interviewed. But at one point he appeared in the doorway and started talking with us. It was clear that he neither wanted to accept any responsibility for what had happened nor, indeed, wanted to admit any special feelings about it.

FRANK:

Don't you find that with most things individuals do, no matter what it might be, they do what they want to do? No matter what. Think about it: marriage, jobs, so forth and so on. Why

41

shouldn't suicide be included? Why should that be someone's fault?

One daughter chooses to go to college, the other doesn't. One might choose to marry, the other not. People make their own decisions. Some make a decision not to live. That's the way I look at it. The end result is the same. Dead is dead.

It was a disease of sorts. I don't have any feelings. She died. I would have felt just as bad if she'd died of a heart attack. It's a loss. Period. It was her decision. I don't feel it would ever happen to one of my two daughters, or that I'd do that. But if they did that, that's *their* problem.

Arlene was only eighteen when her brother killed himself. To everyone's surprise she didn't seem to react at all. That night she went out on a date as usual, despite her parents' objections. For the next month, they could discern no difference in her behavior. She even refused to attend the memorial service, saying that her brother's death was an accident and didn't mean that much to her.

But after a month, she collapsed in school. They took her to the hospital, where she was discovered to have a bleeding ulcer.

*

As we have said, some survivors become overwhelmed by anger, despair, depression, guilt, and anxiety—and others don't. They work their way through and go on with their lives. But it is important for all survivors to understand what they are going through, to recognize the symptoms that are part of grieving after suicide, part of Posttraumatic Stress Disorder, and to recognize when they are stuck in those reactions and cannot move on.

In addition, survivors need to recognize that what they undergo in the first six months after the suicide is only the beginning of the journey. In Part Two of this book, we deal with the middle part of that journey, the Long Run.

Chapter 3

A FAMILY'S STORY

There is no quintessential survivor's story, because there is no quintessential survivor. Each one is different; each one undergoes his or her own ordeal, and then does—or does not—go on with an ordinary life. Throughout this book, where it's applicable, we quote what a wide variety of survivors have to say. But, precisely because those statements come in the context of specific sections of the book, piecemeal, a complete sense of the survivor's life may be missing. To round out the reader's perception of what these lives are like, we twice choose to present an entire conversation with a survivor. Here is the first.

This is a family's story. In it you will find much that we have talked about in the past several pages: the chronology of suicide, the reactions—fears, guilts, angers. Much is missing, too, for no one survivor goes through everything or talks about everything. Finally, there are things that Mildred talks about that we will discuss in some detail in later chapters. Think of this as a precursor to them.

No member of a family sees a suicide quite the same as another. In this family, where there were multiple suicides, that difference in perception is multiplied. In a later chapter, one of Mildred's sons, Sean, talks about the same family suicides. He does not see things the way his mother does.

There were six children. The eldest was Frank, then Sean, Ellen, Audrey, Ernest, and Mac. Eight years ago Frank died of an overdose, which the coroner declared a suicide; two years ago Mac hanged himself. Audrey has been diagnosed as manic-depressive and has tried to kill herself a number of times. But the chain of suicides started with Mildred's husband. Considering everything she has been through, Mildred looks a lot younger than her years. Her language is constricted, uncolored by adjectives, but her story is intense.

It's been twenty-four years since my husband killed himself. I think I "ran" from feeling about it—with six children I didn't have much time. I managed always to keep it at a distance, and I really didn't come to grips with his death. On the other hand, I talked about it constantly, and that was my way of dealing with it. I had an awful lot of good friends. They were all very supportive. One, especially, who lost her husband, and we used to sit by the hours and talk about it. Mostly about the kids: how the death was affecting the kids and what we were doing and how we were trying to cope with being both mother and father for them. Later on I had dreams that my husband was alive and that he wasn't telling me, and I often thought that's how the anger was coming out. I'd see him and I'd say, "Why didn't you tell me you were alive?" and then I'd get furious at him—a couple of years after his death.

He got depressions, but he never missed a day of work. (He owned a gas station; worked seven days a week.) Nobody else knew he was sick. I knew he was depressed, but I used to think it was because of me: what had I done? I'd go along for a while, and then I'd want to shake him, make him talk to me—that kind of thing. I didn't know it was a suicidal depression.

One night, he finished locking up the garage, and there was a sports car that he pulled in, and he hooked it up to a hose. I'd sat up waiting for him and I'd fallen asleep. I woke up. He always called to see if we needed anything, and it was late, so I went down to the gas station; he wasn't there. My father and I waited.

44

It was a full moon, and September, but a warm night. We sat out on the steps. Finally, I went to one of the men that worked for him and banged on the door. I woke his dog up and his baby, but he didn't wake up. Now it was two o'clock in the morning; I went back to the gas station, and it was so quiet that now I could hear the motor running. And I knew, right away. He'd left a note for his doctor that said, "I know *you*'ll understand, but Mildred may need your help." The doctor said, afterward, "I thought he was better than he'd ever been."

I really think I've deflected everything. When anything happened, I worried about the kids. I don't think I ever let myself feel the pain. I had an eighteen-year-old sister die very suddenly, and a twenty-two-year-old sister—of congenital heart failure. So I'd had experience with sudden death, and that was at twelve; I guess you get used to death; you learn coping mechanisms. My father would say, "Things happen. That's God's will." When I hear how other people have reacted, I think I've protected myself against it. When my husband died, the Bay of Pigs was right after that, and I can't remember the Bay of Pigs at all. It's like I forgot about my husband and I forgot everything that happened around that time. I can cry more easily about someone else's family. But you know when I found I cried the hardest? Kennedy died the year after my husband, and I cried for four days straight. I know a lot of people were crying, but I cried and cried and cried. I could let it out for Kennedy where I couldn't let it out for my husband. After Frank died, and then Audrey got really sick, I went to Dr. R. He was a psychologist. He finally told me, "Look, I'm not going to try to make you cry or feel anger; evidently, you've survived the way you have, and that's fine." Because he did try his darndest in the beginning. And it just wasn't there.

Oh, there was lots of guilt! If only I'd understood him better. The business was a strain on him. Maybe if I'd made him get out of the business. I look back, and my husband would come in at night and we'd all be waiting for him. And he'd go out to mow the lawn, and I'd go out and be pacing up and down with him. I look back and say, God, that man must have wanted a few moments' peace! We were married twelve years. And there are always things that you say. Or do. Or don't do. He called that

45

night, and I was down doing wash. He said, "Oh, don't bother, I'll call back later." Only he never did. If only I'd been upstairs when he phoned. . . . As much as I tell myself I understand it as a disease, I feel guilty. My sister told me, "If only you didn't have so many children. I don't think your husband was up to that." That got to me. Then there were rumors after he died: that he was running around; that he was running a numbers racket—well, you have to know my husband. Like my father said, "If he had a mouthful of shit, he wouldn't say it." I mean he was just a real good guy. I laughed over it, it just didn't affect me, those rumors, but I don't know what the kids had said to them in school.

It's funny. We lived next door to the Johnsons. The kids were back and forth all the time. The night my youngest, Mac, died, he called Phil Johnson. And Phil talked to him for two or three hours, and that was the first time Phil knew that my husband had committed suicide. And I always assumed that everyone knew. I figured over the years someone would have mentioned it. He said, "I never knew until Mac told me that night." And then he told me *his* father committed suicide. And *I* didn't know *that.* And Phil still didn't think Mac was serious. He thought he was grandstanding. He'd gotten a gun, and Phil sent someone down to take the bullets away. And then Mac hung himself.

How deeply Mac buried that; all those years it never came out in conversation with his best friend.

Sometimes I don't know whether I've smothered all the guilt and risen above it to another level, or what.

Ellen's had her problems. She was five when my husband died, and she was just so obviously unhappy that I took her to a psychologist and she went for a year or two. And then she was carrying a double major in college and the third year she just called up and said she was coming home, and she's been seeing the psychologist ever since, and that's eight or nine years. She's not depressed, but she claims she's never happy. She was married, but she's been separated for three or four years now. I really worried about her after Mac died. She took his death very hard. I really thought she was suicidal. It was more than she could take. But to look at her you don't know. She's bubbly.

46

Audrey, now, is more like my husband. She just clams up. She's manic-depressive. At sixteen, she just walked out of school. She's on lithium and other drugs. With all the medication, I feel like I've lost her sometimes. I don't know where she is. I think it's had a terrific toll, when you lose your father, your youngest brother, your oldest brother. And they kind of resent me, because I've been able to snap back, and I've had it thrown at me by all of them: "Oh, you're so strong."

We didn't talk as a family until after Mac died two years ago. The thing I found, I would try to talk to the kids about their father, and I would mention his name and, especially Frank, as soon as I mentioned his father, he would walk out of the room. He didn't want any part of it. Then, the night Mac died, I had a meeting with a psychologist and a social worker, but it wasn't Mac they talked about; they all got back to their father. And that was the surprising part to me, you know, the anger they felt. See, I've never been able to feel the anger. Maybe it's buried so deeply. But the kids were angry, they blamed it on me. They hated their father, they hated me, because I must have had something to do with it. This all came out twenty years later.

I just found a letter Frank had written in his twenties, and he said, "I want to apologize for all those things I said about Daddy and you. It was just I was so angry." I used to fight with Frank, because he was a tough one to raise. He had a great sense of humor, though. The last few years with him I began to see the swings. Like Audrey. He'd come in at three in the morning and start talking about his job, then he'd go into a quiet, slow, philosophical stage, just lying there, you'd never hear a peep. And then he'd be on those talking jags. But I don't know whether I could have done anything about it. He didn't think he had a problem.

I didn't understand depression as I do now. I thought if you did this or that, you could change things. I always thought I could keep people alive. It's true; I was holding my breath for years, thinking if I let my breath go, Audrey would just die; she'd give in and commit suicide. I was angry at the whole medical field for not explaining depression to me. When my husband was in the hospital, they asked me a few questions, but they never told me

47

anything. Nobody telling me to try to understand what a depressed person feels. And I wasn't reading any of those articles then. I've read everything since. It's hard for people who don't get depressed to understand that anyone could be in such pain that they'd take their own life. That's one thing Mac said to Phil (I just found this out six months ago): He kept saying, "Phil, you just don't understand the pain. You don't understand the pain." And the one thing my husband said when he attempted suicide once, he said the idea of killing yourself was you *had* to get rid of what was going on in your head.

The older you get, the more you realize that you *may* be able to stop it that day, that time; but what will happen later if they really want to do it?

I have a friend with whom I've worked for fifteen years. We're very friendly. We've worked right together, and someone told me after about five or six years, "I know why you and M. are so close: Her husband committed suicide, too." I *didn't* know it, and I don't know whether she knows I know or not, but she's never mentioned it. I don't think she can even say the word.

I've always told people. I told my children, but I'm not sure it registered. Sometimes I think the younger ones blocked it out. . . . I told all of them at the time . . . Ernest was nine. When someone told him in school, it came like a total shock, but I'd already told him.

They've all reacted differently. Sean used to say about Frank: He was my brother, my father, and my best friend. And, yet, Sean felt a tremendous relief after Frank's death. He'd been sort of "carrying" him. I never had to carry my husband. Like Audrey, who's sick now, she's thirty-one, and I've been carrying her for years. She's attempted suicide many times. I don't know what I'd feel if she died.

I never realized the anger my kids had, until *years* later. That's what I feel sad about. If I'd only realized the anger they were having, then maybe I could have helped. I wish I'd known. I didn't know they were holding that. Frank was so close to his father; to come to grips with his father not being there, and on top of it being a suicide, he just had no place to put it. He was so angry.

And no one ever suggested to me, "Why don't you get the kids into therapy?" after my husband's suicide. That one time I had the meeting, after Mac's suicide, I even thought, "Will they come, will they come?" It's very difficult. Look at Sean. Frank's anniversary was last week, but I gave up asking them to come for masses. I cannot even talk to Sean about Frank. It's going on eight years. And Sean just cannot do it. And yet that night, when Dr. R. was here, he was quite open. He talked on and on. I think he really wants to talk about it. But he can't, with me.

Part Two

THE LONG RUN
"What's Going to Happen to Me?"

Chapter 4

THE BARGAIN: A DEAL WE MAKE WITH LIFE

It's the hardest thing I've ever had to live through. I'll go for a couple of days, and then I'm back to where I was before, and I wonder what it's going to be like in five years. Someone I know who's experienced a suicide told me that the pain eventually gets a little more numb, but I don't know. It just has to be the hardest thing to go through. It's like my own personal holocaust.

—A SURVIVOR

Some of the survivors' emotional reactions are short-term, others go on for years. Some never get shaken, so fierce are the reverberations of suicide. No wonder, then, that under the pressure of this kind of stress, the lives of survivors take on new shapes and forms.

We call the things that people do to deal with suicide *bargains*. Bargains allow survivors to be a little more comfortable with their survivorship. Bargains enable survivors to go on living. We call them bargains because there is a trade-off involved in these deals. The survivor gives up something in return for a more comfortable emotional position. The survivor pays a price and gets something in return. For example:

Scapegoating

In this bargain, the survivor finds one or more people who he or she believes are responsible for the death of the person who actually killed himself. By focusing on the scapegoat, all the anger that might be directed at the suicide or toward oneself goes, instead, to the people chosen as the ones "who could have stopped" the loved one from killing himself or who actually "caused" the death. The intensity of the pursuit of the scapegoat gets in the way of the survivors' living out their lives in a healthy fashion.

Bargains protect survivors against feelings or thoughts that are too painful to deal with. But they also lead survivors into behavior that is harmful to them. In this fashion, a bargain can be said to have costs and benefits. The costs are not always evident. In scapegoating, for instance, the survivor's absence of felt anger comes at a price because that feeling is not really gone. It simply lies buried. And to the extent that the survivor does not accept this feeling as a real part of himself, he does not give himself a chance to talk about it and relieve himself of its burden. The anger stays there, buried, working its poison. Spending the rest of his life attacking scapegoats is likely to render many of his activities unprofitable, to make him bitter, and to cripple him in other ways.

Bad bargains also have a way of keeping people from living out the positive side of their existence: having good marriages (or holding them together), meeting new people, enjoying one's work. The benefit of a bad bargain is that the killing off of a negative feeling allows what is left to move on. If too much is killed off and too big a sacrifice is made, then the bargain doesn't really work. The survivor remains in pain—although it is the pain of being stuck, rather than the pain of unbearable feelings.

What are some more of these patterns of behavior that we call bargains? As you will see, each is different; we've given them names that help to point up some of their features. Here are a few examples. In the chapters that follow we give much more detailed pictures of how the suicide leads to the bargain.

Saying Good-bye

Instead of going on with their lives, some survivors spend years saying farewell to the dead person. A prolonged mourning takes place, without a great deal of pain, but with no forward movement, either.

Guilt as Punishment

Instead of finding an outside scapegoat, these survivors choose themselves. Somehow they feel responsible for the suicide. They become the victim and remain in that role, deep in grief.

Physical Problems

Instead of crippling themselves with psychological problems, survivors may end up with psychosomatic ones. They think they can concentrate on those problems rather than the suicide. Only it doesn't work.

Cutting Off

Survivors may not allow themselves to have anything good in life. As a result, their families may fall apart, divorces occur, people lose sexual drive or lose their jobs. Children are no longer free to act like children, they lose their sense of freedom. One of the researchers in this field discovered that husbands and wives who had lost their spouse by suicide often ended up remarrying someone who was likely to disappoint them again—another way to be rejected by the world, another way of being punished.

Suicide

The saddest bargain of all is that which ends in suicide for the survivor.

Running

Here the survivor keeps moving—from one job to another, from one relationship to another. Anything, rather than face the feelings inside. This leads to denying a lot of good things in life—things that can only be had by staying where we are and working things out—including good relationships with new spouses, or good jobs, or good friends.

And there are other bargains, which we talk about in succeeding chapters.

It is always difficult to determine what people's lives might have been like had they not become survivors. Would they have been depressed anyway? Would they have been divorced, become alcoholics, lost their jobs, had stomach problems, hated their families, been disappointed in their children even if there had been no suicide in their lives? Of course, one cannot know, but what becomes clear in these stories is that the patterns of behavior among family members and friends of people who have killed themselves are indeed dramatic. Taken as a class of people, survivors are victims. They appear angrier, guiltier, and more grief-stricken than the general population. And the bargains they have made—the patterns of adaptation—are clearly costly.

The names we've given to the bargains are simply guidelines to understanding the patterns that underlie them. Like all psychological phenomena the bargains overlap and intertwine. In a final sense, the bargain is only one way of looking at the lives of survivors: a way of telling their stories.

In looking at these bargains it seems to us that anger plays a particularly important role. It is the anger that survivors feel at the dead person that makes things so complicated. That anger is threefold in origin:

It is a rage at being rejected, at being abandoned, and at being accused.

The survivor is rejected by someone who did not consider him important enough to remain living for; abandoned by someone he loved; and accused as if the dead person were pointing a finger and saying, "You didn't do enough for me."

The survivor doesn't know what to do with this terrible anger. It frightens him, makes him feel guilty, makes him feel bad about himself. If we look closely enough at anybody's bargain—we find anger.

Fortunately, bargains are not necessarily permanent. Unlucky survivors get stuck in bargains that are hard to change, leaving them with ways of dealing with the world (and with the suicide) that are harmful not only to themselves but to their families and friends. But if they're lucky, or skillful in finding help, the bargains they make can change over time. This potential for change can be seen in many of the survivors' stories in this book.

And, of course, some bargains help right from the start. Despite anger that is not acknowledged, despite depression and guilt, many survivors are able to keep their lives on the move. In other words, Posttraumatic Stress Disorder and the prolonged grief that accompanies suicide need not be permanently damaging. If we spend a great deal of time in this book discussing the unpleasant bargains that people make with life, it is not to make the survivor's life appear worse than it is, but to label the experiences that so many survivors seem to share. Many people feel that that very labeling helps to make the experiences more manageable. In Part Three of this book we give survivors other techniques that may ease the pain that follows suicide.

Chapter 5

BARGAINS:
THE LONG GOOD-BYE

Most people don't get a chance to say good-bye to the person who kills himself. Suddenness—surprise—is one common aspect of the survivor's experience. Some survivors' bargains, then, involve the effort to say good-bye. Unfortunately, this can mean an endless, unsuccessful effort, one that keeps the survivor in bondage to the dead person. (It may be, in fact, that saying good-bye is mixed in with every survivor's "deal" with life.) The gain here is that if you're still saying good-bye, the dead person isn't quite gone yet—you don't have to experience the loss, fully, yet, and you don't have to express your anger, your guilt, your shame—yet. The cost is that you can't get on with the next business in your own life.

What goes along with this bargain is a sense of isolation. The dead person is gone, a part of you has been ripped out, and you are, in fact, not the same person you were before. If only you could get back to your former state, say good-bye properly, then you could be whole again.

A part of Ruth's bargain seems to be the need to continue saying good-bye (even though Beth's suicide attempts gave her an opportunity to rehearse her farewells). She feels a need to keep her daughter with her; among other things, she has made Beth's bedroom her office. "I feel very comfortable there. It's very much the way she left it. That room holds her memories."

Evan remains very close to Ruth and her family. He visits often. He takes meals with the family as they speak over and over again about the suicide.

EVAN:

I suppose in one sense I'd been saying good-bye for the last three years. But, in another, I have never said good-bye.

Right now I still try to keep her alive. I keep a lot of pictures of her. I take some time every day to think about her; make some time if I don't have it. I continue to come here. I'm very much a part of this family. I sleep in her bed just the way I used to. I find myself talking to her.

It's important to stress that there is nothing inherently wrong with Evan's feelings or his behavior. Survivors have the right—and the need—to express their feelings as they wish. But what are the consequences for Evan of not saying good-bye, of trying to keep Beth alive? Has he killed anything within himself? Is he cutting off a part of his life in return for her death? Does the anger he doesn't appear to experience toward Beth for leaving him find an outlet elsewhere? At himself, perhaps?

EVAN:

I was in a very bad car accident, and I thought I was going to die. I flipped over right on the highway. The thing I most took away from that was when I really thought I was going to die I wasn't disturbed by that fact; I remember vividly thinking, "Well, my time has come, maybe I'll see Beth." Maybe that should worry me more than it does. The only good thing I can say is that in the last five and a half months I've seen myself go through a variety of stages vis-à-vis mourning Beth. There may come a time when I don't want to keep her alive the way I do now. My guess is if my car flips over, I'll do a little more to save myself the next time.

I'm at a point now when it's a crossroads in my life, and it's not very easy to make decisions when my attitude is "What does it matter anyway?" But I realize that I have to do it, because someday it may matter, so I go through the motions. I hope when I find myself in a situation that I will have created by hook or by crook, I'll respond.

I remember way back when the relationship had just started, we were both very insecure. When it was clear we'd become important to each other, one of the things we talked about was who was going to end it first. Each of us was certain the other was. One major regret I have is that I think we were both very special people, and I regret I won't get to live my life with her. Beth ended the relationship first.

Both Evan and Ruth talk about being "wedded to the truth." They are open about their feelings and about what happened. In some ways, they appear to be coping well with the suicide. They made all the arrangements for Beth's funeral and memorial service without falling apart. There is nothing "helpless" about their reactions. But they are also both still struggling with the dilemma of how to let go and say good-bye.

There are a lot of ways of continuing to say good-bye. We talked about Sean when we presented his mother's interview at the end of Part One. He has a different perspective on the numerous suicides and on his mother's response to them. Some of his thoughts are about saying good-bye.

SEAN:

It's almost like a perpetual mourning for her. She always encouraged us to talk about it, but it's like she never *stopped* talking. I mean it's fine, at the right time, but it seems like she's eternally grieving. Ernest came out with a statement: him and her were having a hard time for a while. Once, we went to his apartment. She mentioned another member of the family who had died, and he said, "Jesus Christ, why can't she let the ghosts rest?" Which is the way I feel about it. I mean, I want to get on with my life. I'll give you an example. The day my son was getting baptized (as a favor to my mother), she planned an anniversary mass for my oldest brother. She couldn't understand why no one wanted to come to the mass. For me, that exemplifies mixing up the joy of the present with the pain of the past.

Maybe it's so ingrained into her—death. She'll go to a wake anytime, anywhere. I've seen her turn down so many parties. It's kind of indicative of the way she likes to think. She gets a bigger kick out of a good wake than a good party.

Sean's anger at the multiple suicides in his family often finds its way toward his mother (as we'll see in another chapter) but surely there is something correct in his perception that suicide has killed off some of the joy in his mother's life as she continues to try to say good-bye.

Some survivors spend a great deal of energy trying to avoid the recurring feelings of anger. This makes their saying good-bye only one of many attempts to deal with rage. Their lives often appear to be disconnected, filled with a variety of guilts, angers, and a sense of loneliness. Amanda had a terrible time with her daughter while she lived. But now she remembers her as someone from whom she never wished to part. With a rasping, piercing voice, Amanda seems to be seeking answers with the very tone of her statements. Her face is white, her hair unkempt, and when she is not speaking, she slouches back in the couch, hiding in the pillows.

AMANDA:

Nobody really cares about me the way my daughter did. It's a fact of life. I'm disconnected. I have nobody as far as family, except my cousin, who tells me about her problems with her daughter. You can't talk to people on the outside.

You don't forget. People say it'll get better, but you don't forget. There's something so missing, you feel, and it'll always be there.

I didn't say good-bye. Most of us didn't say good-bye.

She was a beautiful girl—maybe she was too beautiful—one of those breathtaking creatures. I feel guilty about her. I spent twelve years trying to get her off the pills, and it looked like it was going to succeed.

How can I be angry at her when she was so tormented?

How, indeed? That is precisely the dilemma that most survivors face: They do in fact feel angry at the dead person; but they also feel guilty about feeling angry. "How can I be angry at her when she was

62

so tormented?" So the guilt gets reduced by their putting the anger out of sight. Unfortunately, it doesn't go away, and it helps to account for the torment that people like Amanda continue to suffer. If only she could feel better about the daughter who gave her so many problems during her lifetime.

Of course we had problems. I didn't have the energy to be with her twenty hours a day. And the poor thing had the most horrible life, and then she started to come off pills, tried to.

I want to hold her in my arms; I want to have the luxury of taking care of her for three months, for three years, whatever, instead of just like "that." Oh my God, why didn't I pat her head, why didn't I hold her, why did I let her cry? The guilt doesn't go away.

Chapter 6

BARGAINS: SCAPEGOATING

As we have said, all the bargains we'll be looking at have both a positive and a negative effect. Many, if not most, are a way of dealing with the accumulation of rage that builds up both before and after a suicide—rage at the person who died. Overall, the survivor gains by treading water—and denying the anger—while he or she gets a grip on things. But the survivor also loses by not acknowledging feelings. The period of frozen grief can stretch on and on.

While it is primarily the survivor who loses, the fact is that he has relationships with other people. The survivor who damages his own life also damages other people's lives.

My son Albert committed suicide just over a year ago. He had been diagnosed as a schizophrenic, and he had been schizophrenic for five years. He had attempted to commit suicide twice before. Once, on a bridge, he had taken all his clothing off, despite the fact it was November, and he was about to jump into the river when some motorist stopped him. After spending some time in the hospital, he was released.

On January seventeenth, which was a Thursday, there was a heavy snowfall, and I stayed home. At about four o'clock in the afternoon, Albert told my wife he wasn't feeling well and he wanted to go back to the hospital and see the doctor who had been treating him. I asked him what's the matter. He said he was hearing voices.

The man who is telling this story, Erik, is in his early sixties. He keeps his head down during the entire story, his voice subdued, his demeanor depressed; he is on the verge of collapse. He is a school-teacher in a large city. We have the feeling that this story has been told by him in the same manner time and time again. Only when he gets to the doctors at the hospital does his voice rise in scorn and anger.

After five to ten minutes with Albert the doctor called me in. I asked him, "Did Albert tell you he was hearing voices?" "Oh," the doctor said, "he's just hallucinating." "And did he tell you they're telling him to do terrible things?" "That's nothing. I'll give him some pills." I wanted the doctor to put him in the hospital, which was the proper thing for the doctor to do. Instead, he just laughed it off. He said, "He'll take the pills." I have the bottle. I'm suing the doctor and the hospital because they told me to take Albert home.

The next day, Erik went to his teaching job. His son went to the top of a skyscraper and jumped.

This woman called to the guard and told him Albert was going to jump, but the guard refused to come take Albert down. He might have been saved.
As a survivor, I've never forgotten. Can't seem to put it out of my mind.

At this point, Erik bows his head and looks at his feet. His voice drops lower.

Well, that's my story.

66

Later, we learned that Erik is also suing the owners of the building for not having rescued his son before he jumped.

What is extraordinary about Erik is not that he is depressed over his son's death, or that he is angry. What is exceptional is how much energy he is putting into finding scapegoats for his son's suicide and how much energy is being diverted into his own pain. Later in our conversation he says,

> After my son committed suicide, I said I gotta go back to school. So I forced myself, and somehow I was able to do the work, but when June came, I just wanted to die. I didn't want to go on living. I became very ill, physically and mentally. Yes, I felt very guilty about my son dying. I felt that the doctor actually murdered my son, and I wanted to kill him.

The statement about guilt is thrown away, almost as if it has just slipped out, but the anger at the doctor is virulent. What about anger at his dead son?

> I never hated my son. I loved him. I'm not angry at him. I'm angry at myself.

Erik's bargain is to keep alive forever the memory of his son's death. ("I'll never forget.") He kills off the anger he might feel at his son and burns fiercely with anger at himself and at the scapegoats. The price he pays is physical and psychological deterioration. ("I became very ill, physically and mentally.")

Wait a minute, you may say at this point, what's wrong with being angry at a doctor who fails his patient? What's wrong with suing the building? Erik is entitled to justice and to whatever feelings he has. But these are not just feelings, not just a pursuit of justice—this is a bargain Erik has made. And Erik himself tells us—or shows us—what's wrong with it. He has hidden feelings from himself—the terrible anger at his son that he does not acknowledge. And the terrible anger he expresses toward others leaves him unsatisfied. He is in physical and mental anguish.

This certainly seems to be true of Allen, a man somewhat older than Erik. He starts his story by telling us how wonderful his dead daughter

67

was. He harbors no anger at her, nor will he brook any suggestions that she was in any way responsible for her own death. Well educated, with an upper-crust accent, this old and broken man claims attention with his cries.

She was life-loving, fun-loving, people-loving, extremely outgoing, successful in the field she chose. I never had problems with her as a child, either while she was growing or as an adolescent. She had an extremely destructive marriage; we begged, pleaded, we were on our knees, we felt she could not survive this marriage. We pleaded, "Get out."

They went for help, marriage counseling—but her husband is an extremely recalcitrant person. Everything that was said he fought against. He knew better than the counselor, he was marching to his own drummer. She left about five times in twenty-five years, and five times she came back. And it became very very bad. She'd never been emotionally ill in her life, but about a year prior to this tragedy I noticed she was getting very depressed, and she failed to recognize that there was something very wrong with a man who had a pathological need to battle. We begged again. "Get out." She was extremely bright in every area but could not see that he was ill.

Anyway, she became sick enough to be hospitalized. She was not a fighter. She was not able to cope with the constant screaming. She told the doctor, "My house is a war zone, I can't stand it." The doctor sent her home after a while, with medication. She was home about ten days. And that was when . . .

Allen's daughter died of an alcohol and drug overdose. Like Erik, he told the entire story in a quiet, strained voice. A number of times Allen started to cry. Again, we are reminded that it is someone else who is responsible for the death of the suicide. Again, the anger is virulent. But the person who killed herself is not to blame. And yet again, the parent is suffering, both physically and mentally.

I broke down physically, completely. I had an accident. I walk with a cane after surgery. My heart is bad.

At this point, someone suggests to Allen that the pain will lessen, that he may, in fact, forget it. He says, angrily, "I don't want to forget it."

And there it is—his bargain: that he will never be free of the suffering he now feels. But why should he make himself suffer so badly? The answer appears to be that he does indeed feel guilty for what he did, or didn't do, for his daughter.

ALLEN:

When I read about the suicide of a son or daughter, I always say to myself, "Well, there's something that the mother or father of that child did or failed to do in that child's formative years that did not give him or her enough survival strength; that caused him, when the chips were down, to do what he did." I am obsessed with the guilt of that. What did I do or what did I fail to do in these early formative years to give that child the strength for survival, the desire to live? Please tell me, will you?

Someone hastens to reassure him that he was not to blame, that he could not be to blame, that his daughter was a grown woman with a will of her own. But the suggestion is also made that her bad marriage, by itself, could not be the only reason for the suicide. "You don't kill yourself only because you have a bad marriage," someone says. Allen responds in angry tones: "She had no other problems!" And within a few minutes he is backing away from the notion that he, too, might have been responsible. Perhaps the guilt has become too strong for him to manage.

Someone says, "You have a lot of anger in you." And Allen responds, "A hell of a lot! A hell of a lot! When this catastrophe happens, we're all angry at that; we're angry at the people around us who don't support us enough. Do you know, sir, the idiots who are out there? Close friends who say to you, 'It's seven months and you're still crying?' Shouldn't I be angry at them?"

So Allen's bargain includes anger at his daughter's husband, anger at the "idiots" who tell him he should feel better, anger at those who don't support him, and some guilt for what he himself did or did not do. But his daughter, idealized, is not to blame. And he will keep the memory of this pain forever, even if, as it seems to us, that may keep him forever crippled by his daughter's suicide.

It seems appropriate to take up here one of the typical targets for scapegoating: mental health professionals. Almost everyone we talked to had something angry to say about doctors. This *seems* to make sense, because doctors do, indeed, appear to have failed the survivor by not preventing the suicide. Even many of those who are coping with suicide fairly well seemed to be angry at doctors.

Take Sean, for instance:

> My brother and I had the same feeling: that psychologists are just about worthless and that the best ones are when people don't need it, when they're going in for a tune-up. Certainly, state institution psychologists, they're almost parasitic. My sister— they loaded her up on drugs and she never got out of that strain, and I resent it.

Take Amanda. It has been five years since her daughter died, but she just can't shake the feeling of grief, and her feelings about psychotherapy are decidedly ambivalent.

> I resent the fact that my daughter's life was so unhappy. When she came in with an overdose, the doctors would say, "Are you here again?"
>
> Ninety-nine percent of the psychiatrists I saw through her were horrendous. But I go to one sporadically. Lately, I've been going a little more. He may not be the greatest, but, you know, some of these doctors say, "You have to do this, you have to do that," but they're not at all sympathetic. At least he's kind, he seems competent; I can scream and shriek, I can moan.

Anger at doctors comes from a wide variety of survivors, but one of the clearest statements of how it is used as a bargain—to avoid the anger survivors feel at the dead person—came from a woman whose best friend died two years ago. We had come to interview her and some friends. She said, "One of you is a psychologist, right?" Then:

"None of us think much of them, you know; we're pretty angry at doctors." We asked why. "Well, you have to be angry at somebody."

We need to be clear that of course there are mental health professionals who may have failed the family, who were less than competent. But at the same time someone like Mildred makes us aware that *she* knows that she is burying a lot of anger at the suicides in her family and taking it out on scapegoats.

MILDRED:

> The maddest I've gotten is at the medical profession. Maybe that's where I take out my anger. There were doctors in the hospital who really goofed with Audrey. Twice they took her off all medication. And she just went crazy. A padded room and all. I was like a raving maniac. How could they do that to her? She suffers enough. *After* someone's death there's nothing you can do, but here I am, trying to keep someone alive. And they're working against me. I said, "If you don't put her back on lithium, I'll sue you upside down."
>
> I've taken a lot of anger out on the medical profession.

A little bit of scapegoating seems to be practiced even by people who are dealing quite well with survivorship. It helps them with the intensity of the anger welling up inside. Ruth and Evan are good examples.

EVAN:

> There actually was one clearly identified scapegoat in the large picture of the last three years. That was a friend of Beth's at college.

RUTH:

> It was a very tumultuous friendship with a woman that she had, and we still go back to that. If they hadn't met, if she hadn't gone to that college, she might still be alive. It was a very strange, tortured relationship, the nature of which we still don't understand. But Beth's first attempt had directly to do with her friend's behavior in rejecting her; it was the immediate trigger.

71

Like all those whose bargain involves scapegoating, there is some relief for Evan and Ruth in feeling angry at someone other than the dead person. But at other times their conversation also showed how those hidden feelings of anger get in the way of finally coming to terms with Beth's suicide.

Chapter 7

BARGAINS: "I AM GUILTY; I AM A VICTIM"

In chapter 2 we wrote about how much guilt is felt by the survivors of suicide. In this chapter we tell the stories of survivors who seem to have accepted that guilt as their just punishment. They don't fight it. Their lives revolve around it, around their responsibility for the death, no matter how absurd that may seem to those of us who observe them. It is a bargain that places them securely in the realm of the victim. Certainly, by remaining guilty they do not need to acknowledge the anger they feel, but the consequence is that they lose much of the control they should be able to have over their own lives.

We've already met Ruth and Evan. Despite what appeared to be a fairly good adjustment to the suicide and an openness in talking about it, Ruth kept coming back to her guilty feelings.

> I have a very hard time because, of all my children (I have four), the one child with whom I did have uneasiness or conflicts or anything less than smooth and perfect in our relationship was Beth. Dating back to her birth. It's very hard to convince myself that this had nothing to do with her death. I know, intellectually,

on good days, that that alone could not have killed her—that plenty of kids have had much worse mother-daughter relationships and didn't kill themselves—but most days I feel very, very guilty.

I was her mother!

EVAN:

My own feelings depend on the day. There are certain events I would like to have done over again, but basically the way I feel is I loved her very much and I think she knew that, and if I did something on a particular day and wish I hadn't done that . . . I feel that she knew I loved her, I would have done anything for her.

That might have been part of the problem.

RUTH:

That's what you said before—that maybe you were the wrong person for her: loving her too much . . . If you want to find guilt, you're going to find it. [*Very softly*] Maybe you loved Beth more than I did.

EVAN:

That's not true.

RUTH:

Maybe you should blame me.

EVAN:

Plenty of people can blame themselves.

RUTH:

Death by suicide is different from death by anything else. Because she killed herself, I'm terribly focused on her death, and my problems, and her childhood; so many recollections of *bad* moments in our relationship, and I'm trying very hard to get away from this and focus on her life and the beautiful moments we had together and it's very, very hard, and I have such a terrible fear that the longer it takes me to get back to her life, I will eventually forget it, and all I have left will be "what did we do wrong?" "what could we have done?" and it's almost becoming an obsession with me, even though I know I shouldn't be doing it. And I have these moments when I suddenly remember something nice and think about her as if she'd died of leukemia and not of suicide. It's so wonderful. But then I'm back to the bad feelings. That's the legacy of suicide.

To be more precise, that's *Ruth's* legacy of suicide, for not everyone remembers only the bad moments or kills off the good ones; not everyone is so filled with their "responsibility." We tried to find out whether Ruth's guilt came from feelings of anger that she was now turning inward.

> After her first attempt I was so angry I felt like killing her. What a stupid thing to do. To do to *me*. How could you do it to yourself, how could you do it to me? And the second time, the surface reasons were unbelievable: She was preparing for this trip and she got all obsessed about packing. I was just so mad at her. Even while realizing she was very ill.
> But this time I can't generate any anger. I feel so, so, so sad. Maybe it would help if I could feel angry.

But she doesn't. She feels "relief." That, combined with the anger she felt while Beth was alive ("I felt like killing her") may account for the obsessive guilt with which Ruth now seems saddled. Her bargain allows her to remain oblivious to the anger (an anger that might make her feel even worse about herself), but it forces her to kill off the good memories and live with the bad. She has become a victim of her guilt.

We encountered Maria at a self-help group that was meeting in a church. About ten people gathered there every month to talk with each other about those they had lost to suicide. What she had to say was spoken between sobs, in a quiet, strained voice. It was obvious she was in a great deal of pain. What was not so obvious was why, because there appeared to be no valid reason for her to take on so much of the burden of her twenty-one-year-old nephew's death. Yet there was no doubt that she had done so, that she was living with a

75

very real guilt about it, a guilt she shared with the other survivors in her family, but one she took very personally. This guilt certainly made it impossible for her to be angry at the young man who had killed himself. Lips aquiver, tears coming out at every half sentence, Maria is obviously shaken profoundly by what has happened.

MARIA:

I lost my nephew fourteen months ago. He took a gun and shot himself in the head. He did it in his home. My parents lived downstairs, and my brother and sister-in-law and my two nephews lived upstairs. My brother heard the shot, but it was too late by the time he got to the room. My brother had an unlicensed gun in the house, and my nephew put it together and killed himself.

We had absolutely no warning, none of the signs, none of the depression, none of the giving away of possessions.

It's just been a nightmare since. My brother and sister-in-law's marriage was not good before. This has ended it. My sister-in-law and my other nephew moved out of the house. My brother is guilt-ridden and feels like it was his fault because it was his gun. My sister-in-law is blaming him for having the gun there. My parents are devastated. I had a very special feeling for my nephew, and it's just so hard, because we don't know why. I keep thinking *What did we do, what didn't we do, that he was so unhappy? That he had to take his own life?*

The guilt and blame running through this family is evident. But why does Maria feel that she is to blame, that *she* "didn't do" something? We don't know. What we do know is that this appears to be part of a bargain that she made, a response to the death of her nephew, one that leaves her perpetually blaming herself and, by her own admission, unable to move on with her life.

Becoming the victim, sharing the death with the dead person, comes in many forms. One of the more self-aware persons we talked to also seemed to be trapped in that particular bargain. Anne-Marie had a terrible childhood. Her mother was a schizophrenic living in a mental hospital. Her father was also mentally ill; she never knew him. Her brother was put in an orphanage, but he eventually managed to become a successful CPA and lawyer. Then, in his mid-forties, he contracted Parkinson's disease. He was forced to sell his business, to try to work out of his home. The disease got worse.

The Brooklyn accent in Anne-Marie's voice is distinct; she still lives not far from where she was born. Her voice is puzzled, full of pain. The events are recent.

ANNE-MARIE:

After he sold the business, he just withdrew more and more into himself. What haunts me is he'd say, "I'm so lonely, I'm so lonely." He came to my house (my sister-in-law had gone to France for a holiday). It was a normal day. He got up twice in the night; second time he said he wanted to talk about some things. I thought I reassured him. Then the police were at the door.

Anne-Marie's brother had jumped out the window of his bedroom.

I found myself talking to him: "Why didn't you reach out, why didn't you call me? I was in the next room."

What I regret is I didn't follow my own instincts. I was a psychology major. I heard him, but I didn't *listen*. Lately, I've been reading books, textbooks and things, I read everything, and I say to myself, "What am I doing this for, he's dead. What am I searching for?"

I'm paralyzed.

But what is Anne-Marie's bargain? It becomes more clear as she talks about her anger at her brother for leaving her.

I scream, I yell at the window, I look downstairs, I say, "How could you do this to me? We don't have parents, how could you go and leave me? You knew I was all alone." I throw things, I have *hatred* toward my sister-in-law, intense hatred. I'm a very passive person most of the time, and my anger was always low. I have never felt this angry, that I'm in touch with, in my entire life. I'm angrier than I ever was at my mother and my father for not being there. It's so frustrating. Because I always at least had my brother. . . . I don't know. He went out the window *in my house.* Why did he do this to me? Why did he do this to me?

Surely, it must appear to Anne-Marie that her brother did do this to her, for he chose her house in which to kill himself. But instead of allowing herself to remain angry, she vacillates and, in the end, retreats to guilt: She blames herself.

She and her brother were survivors of a previous trauma, the mental illness of her parents. Together, she and he survived that terrible childhood. It almost seems as if they depended on their togetherness in order to survive. Now, he has abandoned her and, naturally, she cannot understand why. For the time being, at least, she puts herself in his shoes. She is the one that failed, not he. By identifying with him, by feeling his guilt, perhaps she doesn't lose him permanently.

That is her bargain. It is a complex one, but its primary value to Anne-Marie is that it allows her to escape her anger when she needs to—an anger from which she might lose her brother forever.

Chapter 8

BARGAINS: CUTTING OFF

Not all survivors' lives fit into neat packages. In this chapter a variety of bargains are described. In all of them the central theme is cutting off. But what is cut off in each case is different. These people have responded to their anger by limiting their experiences across a broad spectrum. There is a poignancy to the way in which each survivor has chosen to impose limits in dealing with the anger and the guilt. There are many lessons the reader can distill from their stories.

Bernice's brother died of a drug overdose eleven years to the day from the time we had our conversation with her. When we saw her, she was working at a center that dispensed information about self-help groups of all kinds. Her psychotherapist had only recently moved to another part of the country, leaving her without the kind of support she knew she needed. She had attempted to kill herself a year and a half ago and had been hospitalized after she had developed Bipolar Affective Disorder (what used to be called Manic-Depressive Illness).

Bernice was congenial and eager to talk. But what struck us was how cut off from her feelings she seemed to be. Bernice agreed.

BERNICE:

When my brother died, my parents didn't want us to talk about it. I wasn't allowed to go to the funeral, so my grief was cut off. My father brought us all together and said Sam's death was "God's way of punishing us" for our sins.

My father is a workaholic. He works at least eighteen hours a day, plus weekends. They're very religious, and that played a large part in what happened after Sam's suicide, because he was into drugs, and my family said he was a disgrace, a curse word.

I had looked up to my brother, so I felt abandoned and unloved when he died. When I developed Bipolar Affective Disorder, I had strong feelings of guilt and depression. Then I took an overdose, but I don't make any connections between my brother's suicide and my attempt.

My psychotherapist said I'm holding on to Sam's death. But the funny thing is I never talked about my brother's death in therapy until just before my therapist left. I really had no feelings about Sam's death until he told me he was leaving. Then I felt a sense of loss. I guess I'm not in touch with my feelings.

We asked Bernice if, working at a self-help clearinghouse, she'd gotten involved with any of the mutual-support groups that are beginning to form around suicide survivors. After eleven years of cutting off her feelings about her brother's suicide, wouldn't that be a helpful way to open up?

BERNICE:

I'm afraid to go to a group, to let emotions come out and be with strangers.

You know, when I was in the hospital, I met a lot of "druggies." I had been relieved that my brother died, because I thought he was better off that way, but when I met those addicts in the hospital, I realized that they could be helped, that they're nice people. Now I feel guilty that I was relieved about Sam.

We've already heard Sean talk about his family in chapter 5, but only in relation to his feelings about his mother's unwillingness to say good-bye. Here, in a longer excerpt from his conversation, is his perspective on how he and his family have reacted to the multiple suicides in their lives. Sean works in a machine shop. He is lean and laid-back. Not long ago his ancestors lived in County Cork and spoke a rich brogue. One can almost hear it as he pours out his feelings.

SEAN:

Well, I've sure seen a lot of action in that department.

If I feel anything, it's a sense of emptiness. It's too bad I didn't know my father, but I don't really feel I can blame anyone for his death. I thought, earlier, I might have had something to do with it. When I was very young, we had these super-eight home movies. My mother was taking pictures; my father was trying to get me into the frame. I elbowed him around. I remember looking at that later and thinking, "Oh my God, what did I do to my father?" But that was at an early age.

In '62–'63, that was the psychedelic period, both my older brother and I were into some heavy drugs. My will to live at that point wasn't very good. I thought, if I make it to twenty, I'll be lucky. I was heavily influenced by my brother. I looked up to him.

I felt a lot of anger in more recent years at my father for creating this whole mess. I do think his death is instrumental in destroying our family. And in my more rational years, from my twenties on, I did have an anger with him. I had a hard time calling him father. Deep down, I guess, I am bitter. He wasn't a father to me in many ways. Of course, he provided for me; the fact that I never saw him was because he was providing for me. In that way, I respect him, but I do think he could have given it a better shot.

And I did feel angry at my mother for not providing some sort of fertile ground for my brother. She should have known to get some help: He was sick. I resent her for not having some insight into how sick he was, that he needed some stability in his life. He didn't need to be fighting at that age. He should have had a companion, some sort of substitute father. She could have gotten remarried. That certainly would have provided some stability.

Both of us were into hard drugs for a while, but Frank got psychologically into them more than I did. That's what killed him.

81

That last night, he was on drugs and alcohol. The insurance company did not want to pay. They considered it a suicide. Something very strange happened between us; in a way, I blame myself for his death. (Not wholeheartedly. I accepted he would die at some point anyway, and I thought I would, too.) We were very close, and there was this girl I was in love with, and it probably wasn't in my best interest, and I think he saw that. And he was trying to put a wedge in between us, probably for my own good, and I resented that. One day, when we really got plastered on vodka, I said something nasty to him, I don't remember what. He never told me what I said to him, but we were strangers for a month after that, and within a month after that he was dead. I think it led up to his death. Not that you can say something to someone that kills, I don't mean in that sense, but I'm still curious: Whatever it was I said, it was traumatic to him.

Sean is, at best, ambivalent about responsibility for his brother's death. The anger he might feel at yet one more family member abandoning him (the brother with whom he was extremely close) seems diverted into guilt, and he seems to have cut himself off from some potentially productive parts of his life.

I don't think I've lived up to my potential. I mean by potential—right after high school I didn't know what I wanted to do, so I wanted to take a year off, but I was pressured into going to college. That's another thing I resent my mother for. I had three years at Fordham, taking religious courses, English, and so what? At the time I was thinking I should have gotten into business, something that might have led into accounting or engineering. When I'm fifty-three, if I'm doing the same thing I'm doing now, I won't be happy.

May and her husband, Ralph, are both the victims of more than one suicide. Their fathers killed themselves when Ralph and May were young, their brothers killed themselves thirty years later. We've encountered them before (in chapter 1, May described how she was present on Christmas Day when her father killed himself). Now in her early sixties, May sits in a wheelchair, crippled by a muscular disease.

She and Ralph are happily married and seem to have made a wonderful support team for each other. At the same time, she seems aware of many times in her life when her feelings took control of her and ways in which she has been cut off from a more productive life for herself. There is a serenity to May. Whatever anguish she feels is not reflected in her voice or face.

We didn't see much of my mother for a month or more after my father's suicide. She was not in very good shape physically and she had quite a breakdown and we went to stay with friends. We went to his funeral—my two brothers and I were together for that—and then I don't know how it happened, but we were split up, and that I think was terrible. I guess my brothers stayed together, but I went with friends who wanted to adopt me. My mother said, "No, this is enough," and brought us back home and we stayed in that house for maybe six months and then moved away. You know, just moved completely. My mother talked about it a lot to me. My brothers and I talked some, but not an awful lot; when we were smaller. As adolescents I think we talked very little about it—very little. Then my older brother also committed suicide, and so the middle child and I have talked certainly more since then.

My mother went through every stage of blaming him, blaming herself, blaming everybody. I don't know whether I had any feelings of guilt that I didn't stay with my father that night. I don't think so, but maybe I did.

My mother went over and over what she should have done differently and what he had done to her and what their life had been like—first he was the greatest man in the world and then he was a terrible man. I hated her when she talked badly about him. I was hard on her in my mind. Not out loud. I never discussed that with her because she was a very strong, fierce woman. I never got into any confrontation with her.

But I was sure it was her fault. And anger at him: You know, why did he *leave* me? I was his favorite and why should he have left me and then why did he do it the way he did, so that I was bound to find him?

I can't think that he would have done it deliberately to hurt me. I don't believe that. I'm pretty sure I'm not just covering up for him or anything, I think he had financial worries, and there were worries about another woman who was making trouble, all this kind of thing. He'd tried it many times before that, and we knew he had. We saw him.

I went through an awful lot of stages. I became very religious. I went to many different churches, looked very hard to find a religion that pleased me. Finally, I stopped, mostly because of physical difficulties, I think, otherwise, I'd still go. It was a way of trying to find a way of life.

I did dream about him an awful lot and I still do: just recently I had an insight into an awful series of dreams that I've had for years of being in a house with lots of doors and going from one room to another and fear of something in a room. There's something behind a door, which, of course, is exactly what happened. But it took me a long while to realize what that dream meant. In the dream I would keep opening one door. It took me until just a couple of years ago—I'm sixty-one—before I understood it.

Fears? Oh, yes. I know that I always had the feeling that any man I was associated with was going to leave and I realize that after a while I would push him away. Still today, if Ralph is out sailing and he's much later than he said he would be, I'm sure he's not coming back. I still do that.

I wish I had had psychotherapy. I think that I would have been . . . I would have had a much happier adolescence. I think I was a very unhappy girl. I was very lonely. I did nothing but read. I escaped into reading. I would read two and three books a day sometimes. I think I was a very unhappy child.

May says she was angry at her father, but then she immediately "corrects" herself by pointing out that he had financial and marital difficulties; perhaps he couldn't help himself. Her unhappy childhood resulted in part from having to reconcile these contradictory feelings, from burying her anger.

Some bargains are malleable, open to change; they don't seem to hinder the survivor a great deal. These "lucky" survivors nonetheless often make small sacrifices along the way in order to deal with their anger.

Wanda, a family therapist in her early thirties, expressed her feelings openly during our conversations. She had energy, and one felt her emotions were close to the surface; she seemed to have gained a great deal of control over her pain by talking about the suicide. Nevertheless, she noticed that in some areas of her life she was still unable to function the way she wanted to. She was still reacting to her father's suicide with a bargain or two.

It was August—a year and four months ago. It's still not entirely real to me. My father was seventy. He was living by himself, but he had a very nice woman friend. (It was like a nice older-couple relationship.) She had her house, and he had his, but they were very well suited. I was the youngest, I was the daughter, and he always took care of me. It was a close relationship, but he didn't confide in me the way he did in my older brother.

A number of things happened: His oldest brother died suddenly, and that hit him hard. Then the same day he went in for a pacemaker operation. He was always a very avid tennis player, kind of a macho guy, and that was very hard for him. Then, there was this woman who had been hounding my father for over a year to sell our house. My father was the last remaining one in the house; we'd lived there for thirty-five years. My father was a very sympathetic guy and he said he'd give her a very low price. He didn't want to sell it, but she'd been hounding him, and I think probably almost took my father's hand and guided it on the dotted line. Everyone was telling him to get rid of the house, except for me, which he told me in the last conversation I had with him. Anyhow, I called him one morning before I went to work (because I hadn't heard from him), and my father sounded to me like he was under so much pressure. He said, "I sold her the house and now I want to get out of it and I don't know what to do, and she won't let me out of it. I'd like to kill myself." It was weird. It was not him. So, needless to say, I just about fell off my chair and I called my brother. There was a lot of denial in my family operating around this. My brother called my father, and then I talked with him, and he denied that my father sounded that bad. Now I thought that was nuts!

Anyway, I talked with my father that night and I told him that he had said he wanted to kill himself and I said, "Dad, I don't want you to kill yourself." He said, "Oh, I wouldn't do that to you." And then he said something like, "I don't want to move," and I said, "I know. I don't blame you, you've been in that house a long time." And I still remember this—it was the last conversation that I had—he said, "You're the only one that understands."

I had talked with my uncle about flying home, and I didn't. Why didn't I fly home when I knew my father was in distress? I could have done something, or, even if I wouldn't have been able to do anything, at least I would have made the effort. It's something that I'm just going to have to learn how to live with.

I got a call that following Tuesday on my answering machine that my father had killed himself. He had asphyxiated himself in the car. My oldest brother found him. I think my father had stayed up all night—it was the day of the closing of the house—and he didn't go. He was backed into a corner. He didn't know what to do. He couldn't move, and this bitch would not release him from the contract.

I was tremendously angry at my father for a long time. I remember the night that it happened. Friends of mine came over, and I remember that I almost put my fist through the bathroom wall. I really almost did. I just remember pounding the bathroom wall. I was so furious at him for not waiting.

I don't think I've felt angry at him for a couple of months. But I think I still have some deep hidden (from myself) anger at my oldest brother. He was closest to my father and could have done differently than he did. I haven't said this to him and I probably won't. But I found out later my father had sent out a lot of signals that my brother deflected. My father had said, "If I had a gun, I'd shoot myself." I never knew that.

Since my father's suicide, I have had this anxiety that somebody else in my family would commit suicide, and I still have it if anybody gets too upset, like my brother.

Wanda's bargains are minimal: She has picked a scapegoat (the "bitch" who wanted to buy her father's house); and she continues to bury some of her anger and guilt toward other family members, including her dead father. In short, she cuts herself off from some of her feelings in order to go on with her daily life. But, on the whole, her bargain seems more positive than negative.

But sometimes a survivor very clearly cuts off emotions that would make his or her life more peaceful. Barbara, a woman in her fifties, divorced, with some medical problems, and bringing up three adolescents, is aware of this bargain in her life, of the feelings that have no place to go. But she is also having a difficult time changing; her father's suicide has left her with some terrible dilemmas.

Endlessly chain-smoking, Barbara suffers from a hoarse voice. Her sentences are long, held together with *uh*s. She seldom looks at us as she talks, and she seems to be drifting off into the past as much as she is talking about the present.

My mother died in 1968, and Amy, my daughter, was born in 1969. Then, in 1970, my second child was born, and I think it was four months after my second child was born that my father committed suicide. I had a third child who was born in 1972. That goes to the heart of my feelings: I was very angry at him.

He was about sixty-four, and he was very depressed and very closed and secretive, and he was very close to my mother, so when she died, we knew that he had lost the primary hold he had on reality. There really was no reason—for him—to go on living.

I felt very angry. And I still do. Everything was out of kilter, because I had my children when I was in my forties, so all my relations had died and my children never had any relatives. I was furious with him.

I think it really scarred my brother—he had a lot of complicated feelings about it, which he never did really work out, and he wouldn't talk about it. He became depressed and then he became all removed. It was hard to relate to him, and we were afraid he was becoming like my father. His wife was having a lot of anxieties about it, so she talked to me about it, and I would visit him and I would talk to him but I could never reach him. He died. He had a brain tumor, suddenly.

I think that I had the feeling of anger and I've used that feeling of anger to shut out all other feelings, and I was aware of that at the time and I thought this is a good thing to do because

87

I have to raise these children. I was having troubles with my husband, and I didn't think the marriage would last and I pretty much thought I would have to bring the children up on my own. So I felt I couldn't take on—in a sense—the luxury at that time of letting all those other feelings out. So I used the anger, I let the anger come out very strongly, and I think I repressed the other feelings. It was very effective.

What feelings did she not acknowledge?

Oh, I assume, loss! For myself.

It would have been very different if I had had no children, no demanding role that I had to play. I was on my own. That's a very physical act. I was exhausted. I don't think I had time for the first seven years to even think about it.

Barbara is a very intelligent woman. She is aware that she "parceled out" (cut off) her feelings; she sees that she didn't let herself experience the loss or the anger for herself, but for her "children's sake." But she doesn't seem to be aware of the cost to herself of holding it all in. She is suffering physically; she is suffering emotionally. And she stayed married longer than she should have (by her own admission) because she didn't acknowledge the anger that her *husband* deserved. She seems to think this balancing act would have been even harder if she had allowed herself all her true feelings. It is a bargain of which she seems aware—but she ignores its consequences.

I think I might have different feelings once I'm on my own, with the children grown. I have to keep this little merry-go-round going around here. If I had been on my own, it would have been much more complicated.

Barbara has, in fact, made matters more complicated, not less, by cutting off her feelings, by insisting on this complex balancing act; she herself does, in fact, have some suspicion that something is not right with her bargain.

There was this schoolteacher, a very organized woman, rigid almost, and her daughter killed herself. She fell apart, she couldn't go on with the show. There's something about this that's interesting for me. Someone who's so rigid all her life, and this was the one instance where her mechanism broke down. She just completely immersed herself in grief; can't focus, can't pull things together. I guess what I'm saying is how could *I* put that aside where my father is concerned? What happened to *my* grief?

Chapter 9

BARGAINS: A MISCELLANY

WHY?

SARAH:
  I still want to know why she killed herself.

FRANK:
  The end result is the same. Dead is dead.

SARAH:
  But why *then?* That night. I want to know!

Why? is often the first word that comes to the lips of survivors. It may remain there for many years—perhaps forever. You hear it from the moment the suicide happens: "Why did he do it?" "Why did she leave me alone?" "What made him think we didn't care?" "Why, why, why?" It is a natural, if endlessly frustrating, task. Natural, because survivors need some kind of reassurance, some way to eliminate the possibility that *they* were the reason for the suicide. Frustrating, because only the dead person has a clue as to the real reason why. Everything else is surmise, guesswork, self-blame, accusations. And yet, almost all survivors go through the roster of possibilities, over and over again.

Why? is a question asked not only by survivors. Psychologists, psychiatrists, social workers, concerned government figures, and the general public have all wondered why. Scores of books and articles, Ph.D. theses, and tracts have been written about why people commit suicide or why people attempt suicide.

And answers can be given: depression, Bipolar Affective Disorder, stress, hostility toward a family member, hostility toward oneself, schizophrenia, old age, alcohol, and so on.

Judging by the endless repetition of the question on the part of survivors, however—many of whom have been told, or have read about, these "answers"—they do not satisfy the quest. A survivor may be able to say, "My sister was depressed," but he also continues to utter the words, "Why did she do it?" A survivor can say, "Dad was angry at the world," but she also has to say, "I don't understand." A family can say, "We were hostile toward each other," but it still wants to know "Why? What is the whole truth?"

In part this is because the question *why?* can be translated into a different kind of query: What was there in my loved one's life that made it so unbearable? Was I partly responsible? What could I have done to make him happier? Could I have kept her from dying? In short, *why?* can be a shorthand way of expressing guilt.

Maria, whose brother had killed himself only three months earlier, is one of those survivors for whom *why?* seems especially important. She is relentless in her search for a reason for his death.

> I've been reading books, I go to all the bookstores. I read everything, textbooks and all sorts of things, and I say to myself, "What am I doing this for? He's dead. What am I searching for?"

Survivors who spend endless hours asking *why?* may be asking a bona fide question: "Why did he do it?" But they may also be avoiding the discussion of guilt and anger that would make them even more uneasy. Maria's search may actually be a search for a way to undo what has happened. And that, sadly, is impossible. So she makes do with *why?*

There are some survivors who ask *why?* forever. They pursue every avenue. No stone is left unturned. Relentlessly, ferociously, endlessly, they must get to the bottom of the mystery. Was it biochemical? Was it genetic? Did the husband or wife or son or father or niece have a reason? What was it? Can we find it out? Was there a note? Does it explain anything? The problem with the endless search for *why?* is that it takes up too much time. It interferes with relationships; it gets in the way of getting on with life.

It is, of course, reasonable to want to discover if there was a specific incendiary moment—something that sparked the final suicidal desire. It is reasonable to ask if a hidden disappointment or obstacle made someone die. It is even reasonable (though frustrating) to try to imagine what personal failure led the dead person to kill himself. But it is neither reasonable nor healthy to go on searching forever, keeping *why?* in the forefront of one's existence, pushing the question and the search ahead of one like a minesweeper.

The person who relentlessly pursues *why?* is probably refusing to acknowledge that there was no rational reason for the suicide. And the search for *why?* helps disguise the anger, guilt, and shame inside the survivor. The search for reasons—a consuming passion—becomes a shield, but one that turns the survivor's life into a frustrating, fruitless quest.

RELATIONSHIPS

Families break up over suicide. What a pity that is. At the very time that people really need each other, the shock of the event kills off some of the love and respect they had for each other, replacing them with bitterness and anger. In our conversations we heard about blame, we heard about anger, divorces, demands for reparations. Anne-Marie, whose brother killed himself in her house, finds that getting back together with her sister-in-law and the niece she cares about seems almost impossible.

> She doesn't talk to me anymore. I've lost my niece. I'm kind of waiting for the right moment to make contact with them. Am I going to be rebuffed by the child, too? What has she told her?

It always comes to sides. I sided with my uncle over the money. And why did I side with him? Because of love. He put me through college; he took my brother out of the orphanage, brought him up, put him through law school. Loved him. And on top of that, he visits my mother in the hospital, after forty-three years. Tell me: What right does she have to put me in that position? She blames everyone.

And if relationships come apart, it's also hard to put new ones together.

WANDA:
I found that I could not establish any new relationships. I started going out with somebody before my father died, and afterward they tried to take up the relationship, but I couldn't get to know somebody when I was in the process of saying good-bye.

MAY:
I know that I always had the feeling that any man I was associated with was going to leave and I realize that after a while *I* would push them away.

SARAH:
I do have trouble with other relationships . . . with girlfriends. I'm very skeptical. I thought I knew my mother so well, but I couldn't see her suicide coming the night before it happened. So how am I going to know with an outsider?

On close examination some family breakups and relationship difficulties turn out to be survivors' bargains. Suicide is the ultimate rejection, and in its aftermath, sometimes, in order to keep from being rejected again, *we* do the rejecting. It's not a profitable bargain, because we end up being alone anyhow—and feeling rejected anyhow.
But the bargain can be worse than simply controlling new relationships, controlling rejection. There are husbands and wives who, after the death of their spouse by suicide, choose a new partner who exhibits equally unhealthy personality traits: an alcoholic, a wife beater, or even another suicide. For children, it can be even

more severe. Their father or mother abandons them, violently, willingly, by suicide. They grow up, but how can they learn to trust again? Better to reject all suitors; that way *they* won't be rejected, so they think. As adults, time after time, they end relationships that could be healthy and supportive—because they have learned never to trust people again.

There are some survivors for whom the ability to establish any new relationship is not tied to a bargain but to the all-consuming nature of their sorrow and grief. Such people often seem actually physically stunned by the suicide of their sons, daughters, friends, and brothers. Their bodies are bent over, not from age, but from grief. Many of them suffer from physical ailments. They speak in low, depression-ridden voices, and weep as they recite the litany of the suicides: a repetition of facts, with little change from day to day. They are stuck, frozen, riddled with grief. There seems to be no possibility of such people finding any satisfying relationship in their lives.

CONTROL

When a parent dies, children often feel utterly helpless, unable to stave off any future blows the world may deal them. Paradoxically, they may simultaneously feel as if they caused the death. (We go into this in some detail in chapter 16.)

One of the results is that children try to take too much control over their lives and their feelings, as if they could counter the disaster that has struck *after* it has happened. Dave, who was nine at the time his mother killed herself, falls into that category. From the very beginning, he exercised remarkable control over, first, his feelings, then his behavior.

When we interviewed him, he was twenty-five, having already spent an extraordinary amount of energy learning about mechanics and electronics—things that would allow him to "control" or "fix" the world around him—and we noticed how often Dave emphasized the need for control in his description of his feelings after his mother's death. But, of course, nothing could "fix" or reverse his mother's death.

My mother killed herself by inhaling fumes from the car. She went out and she parked the car and she connected a hose to the exhaust pipe and brought it in through the car window. I believe that it was the following day that I found out how she killed herself. I remember wondering what other people would say, what I should say to other people.

I spent quite a bit of time over the next few weeks by myself. My friends would never bring the subject up. They were afraid to touch it. I really didn't talk about it too much with my brother and sister. Sometimes, when they felt like talking, I'd sit there and listen, but I didn't volunteer any information, or ask too many questions.

I sort of leaked out emotions to myself, let myself think about how I felt little by little; I didn't really cry much or anything. Little by little I thought about it, at a rate that I felt I could handle at the time. One thing I recall now was with all the great intentions people had, how much it hurt every time someone sent a sympathy card. I didn't want to think about it. At school, in all my classes, all my classmates had signed a sympathy card; it was like the last thing I wanted.

I would say I had some amount of depression, but most of my feelings didn't come out until two or three years after; that's when I started missing her the most, when I started thinking about how much different summer vacations were; or going skiing without her.

Maybe I feel as if I'm somewhat of a unique person in how I've handled it, like the fact that I leaked feelings to myself.

Dave is, at present, a superintendent in a housing complex. His father is a teacher of physics and his mother was also a professional, working with disturbed children. Dave's bargain cuts him off from many of his intellectual capabilities, his feelings, and much of his potential. In his effort to control his life he has given up some of its possibilities.

SAVING THE WORLD

He never felt he had accomplished enough. Every day was the symbol of another failure.

Jeremy, a successful research physicist, is talking about his father, a lawyer, who had racked up quite a fortune in the twenties and thirties, first in the practice of criminal law, then in civil law. By the time Jeremy's mother killed herself in the late 1930's, his father had a six-bedroom house on seven acres in a fashionable suburb and a large law practice. After the suicide, however, things changed.

At the beginning, he was just depressed. Then, one Saturday (he usually worked Saturdays), he told us he was quitting law. We were surprised, because we thought he knew everything about the law and couldn't understand why he would change jobs. Of course, I was only seven, and my sister was nine, so we didn't concern ourselves with things like that.

He went to work for an organization that specialized in promoting change in laws that dealt with juvenile delinquents. Years later, I learned that he got paid only a dollar for the first year. It was that important to him to be doing that kind of work! What they did was to look at the way delinquents were treated and then see if there wasn't some relationship between that and all the adult crime going on. Dad had this crazy idea that you could actually eliminate crime by finding out what made young people become delinquent, and then by changing the laws (if they were to blame) or other things in society (if the blame fell on them).

He didn't have much time to be with us, or much money to buy things for the family. He was always down at the office, trying to save juvenile delinquents. Of course, now, I'm ambivalent about it: I see the good he did. For instance, he was responsible for the law that made it illegal to put kids under sixteen in jail with older criminals. But at the time, I was angry that he didn't spend any time with *us.*

His attitude about the world was strange. I remember, when I was in high school, getting a chance in my senior year to apply for a summer job where I could travel in Europe. It was a very exciting notion, and I worked like hell to write my application. One day Dad took me aside and said, "Don't get your hopes up. The world doesn't always reward those who deserve it, you know." I allowed as how I still thought it worth applying. He shook his head, as if to say, "How stupid young people are." What he did say was, "I just want you to be prepared for the worst."

I never got the feeling he was happy with anything *he* did, either. Every time he got a new law passed or got people to pay attention to juvenile delinquency, he was always putting himself down. It wasn't *enough*. Finally, after ten years at that, he up and quit.

Then he went to work for a civil rights organization. He was going to eradicate racism in America. I mean, I think he really believed that. But he still didn't see himself as accomplishing anything, even when he went in front of the Supreme Court to argue a case—and won!

And he'd started to drink. A lot. I guess he was a regular alcoholic. I remember trying to talk about it with him. He was furious with me. None of my business. But you could tell he wasn't happy with his life. And the peculiar thing was, he was damn good at what he did. But it never seemed to him that he was doing enough.

Of course, Jeremy's father wasn't doing enough, not in his terms. His agenda was to make up for his wife's death. He hadn't been able to keep her from killing herself, so he would change the world. Or so he thought.

This isn't an isolated case. Two of the psychologists who have spent some time researching survivors' reactions, Albert C. Cain and Irene Fast, have found that, among a group of spouses whose husbands or wives had committed suicide, the sense of rejection posed by the dead person's patent decision to leave them and their world, the irrational, intense guilt experienced by the surviving spouse, the silence that surrounds the suicide, the lack of support (indeed, the blame) from friends and relatives, all lead to an array of personality problems, among which is the "world-rescue" pattern. Cain and Fast say that such people appear to want to make up for the spouse's death by accomplishments such as

> grand economic designs, cancer cures, ultimate paths to religious experience, inoculations against mental disease, food production from special substances to feed the world's population, and the like. . . . these pursuits increasingly expanded, eventually becoming a total preoccupation, a near fanaticism, to the detriment of the person's other interests, activities, responsibilities, and professional reputation.

These goals become unreachable fantasies that can only disappoint the survivor and make his or her world seem painfully empty.

On a less global level, but allied to the world-rescue fantasy, Cain and Fast discuss surviving husbands and wives who marry chronically ill or handicapped people after the suicide of their spouse, in an obvious effort to play out the role of "savior" or loving spouse. The surviving husband or wife is willing to sacrifice his or her happiness in an effort to show how "good" he or she is and to "repair or undo" the damage in other human beings in order to undo the damage that was done to the person who killed himself.

JEREMY:
My father's third marriage, seven years long, was to a woman who was a drug addict. We asked him why he stayed married, since they seemed to have nothing in common. He said, "I feel sorry for her. I'm going to wait until she gets on her feet before I leave her." But his drinking got worse, and so did her drug use.

Sometimes, the need to marry someone with whom a survivor can demonstrate his "goodness" comes not only out of the guilt survivors feel but out of the additional burden—as if there weren't enough—laid on him by neighbors and relatives that he "drove" his spouse to suicide. This terrible notion reverberates throughout such survivors' lives, adding to the self-inflicted guilt they already live with, the silence they force upon themselves and others, and the aborted mourning process. It is bad enough to lose a husband or wife to suicide without having to bear the burden of being told by the dead person's relatives or your neighbors that you are responsible. And yet it happens.

SEXUAL UNHAPPINESS

What can we say about sexual activity among survivors? Only that it is as prone to being "killed off" as are other feelings and activities.

Laurie was a healthy woman in her early twenties when her father contracted cancer. As the disease progressed, it became apparent that he could not be cured. After a discussion with his wife and the older sons and daughters, excluding Laurie ("They felt I was too young"), her father took an overdose of sleeping pills. This "rational suicide" was said to be understood by the family and close friends as necessary, but Laurie was incensed. "How could he abandon me like that?" She went into a depression, her anger turning inward. After some therapy and work with a self-help group, she went back to work, apparently recovered. "But I was dead sexually. Even this one man whom I had been seeing didn't interest me. No one did." Her depression returned.

Laurie's bargain allowed her to go on with the rest of her life, but she had cut herself off from the sexual pleasure that had previously been part of her healthy self.

TIMOTHY:
  There just doesn't seem to be anyone who I like enough. I meet a woman, and she seems perfect. We date a few times, the sex is great, and then I lose interest.

It's not an unusual story, told about some young men or women as they enter adulthood. But Timothy is in his thirties, and this has been going on for years. His sister killed herself when she was nineteen and Timothy was fourteen.

  We weren't that close because of the age difference. She had boyfriends when I was still in elementary school. When I got to high school, she was in college and then, suddenly, she killed herself. No one knew why. My parents were unable or unwilling

100

to talk about it. I had tremendous tantrums in high school and I got disciplined a lot. I missed her. Even though we hadn't been close, we liked each other. She had promised to go out with me on a double date when I got into college.

Timothy did well in college, majoring in economics and getting a job on Wall Street right after graduation. He is a tall, good-looking man and says that he was always well liked.

That wasn't the problem. Women liked me, but I could never find anyone I could fall in love with, and after two or three dates, I became impotent . . . it was very embarrassing. I'd come on like gangbusters, we'd have a terrific time, but then I couldn't get any sexual feelings. I must have dated a hundred girls and broken up with them all.

MEDICAL AILMENTS

While these, in and of themselves, are not necessarily bargains, they are often part of bargains. Survivors suffer from a multitude of medical problems. Researchers have reported for a long time on survivors' alcoholism or drug addiction or their psychosomatic symptoms. We heard about headaches and sinus problems, stomach ailments, heart attacks, and more. Some psychologists feel that the more intense sufferers are not just reacting to the death of their loved one, but to their own guilt. Physical and mental illness become a way of punishing oneself for the loved one's death, or of identifying with the dead person. If a survivor is angry enough, he may turn the punishment around on himself.

And, in fact, many survivors are acutely aware that their health has suffered as a direct result of the suicide. People like Erik and Allen (chapter 6) are prime examples. What even these survivors don't recognize, however, is that the debilitating medical problem is intimately tied to the anger they are unable to acknowledge. The body responds, even if the conscious mind doesn't.

Our conversations leave little doubt that suicide survivors' bodies react adversely as part of the deal the survivors are making with life.

Chapter 10

THE SADDEST BARGAIN: "BECAUSE YOU DIED, I'LL DIE"

Those left behind are faced by a triple loss: that from death, rejection, and disillusionment . . . suicide takes away self-worth. All these factors operate to increase the potential of hostility in the mourner and the danger of his turning it upon himself as the only available or most appropriate target.
—ERICH LINDEMANN AND INA MAY GREER

"I feel like killing myself."

Hardly any survivors escape the impulse. In some sense it is the survivor's worst nightmare. The impact of a loved one's death makes him feel worthless and leaves open the fear that he, too, will commit suicide. The fact is that many survivors do. It is the saddest bargain.

There are claims that suicide among survivors is between 80 and 300 percent higher than in the general population. In our own work, about one-third of the families we talked to had more than one suicide within succeeding generations. If migraines, alcoholism, stomach ailments, and numerous psychological problems follow a family member's suicide, so might suicide itself.

If it's clear that there sometimes is a pattern to the suicides in families, it's not so clear how to predict which survivor will follow in the footsteps—a true victim of the dead person—and which will not. The likelihood is that each case is distinct, each supplying its own reasoning. One person idolizes the dead person and wishes to follow in her footsteps; another feels lost and depressed without the father whom he never really knew; another punishes herself; another suffers from the same biochemical ailment; and so on. If only we could talk to the survivor and ask, "Why did you choose to be the ultimate victim of someone else's suicide?"

It may be that a variety of factors operate to push a survivor in the direction of suicide, and we are left without knowing which may be the crucial one. Was the survivor also suffering from Bipolar Affective Disorder? Did a sister's suicide give "permission" to the remaining members of the family to follow suit? (Someone who was admired dared to commit suicide; now the rest of the family can do it.) If we can rid ourselves of anger at the dead person by finding scapegoats, we can also turn that anger in on ourselves. In fact, many researchers find that the survivor is constantly turning the anger and hostility he feels at the dead person upon himself. Guilt and depression—and suicide—can often follow. We can even create an idealized picture of the dead person, identify with him and want to be like him, down to the very suicide itself.

Ruth's daughter, Beth, left behind a suicide note that, in form and substance, was very similar to that of an aunt who, twelve years earlier, had also killed herself.

RUTH:

She was close to her aunt, closer than we realized. After my sister-in-law died, we asked Beth to come to the house and we helped out my brother-in-law and the kids. We did the cooking. He wanted her clothes out of the house right away, so Beth helped me with that and she was aware of the suicide note. We found out later that Beth had copied the suicide note verbatim, and I also found tremendous similarities between Beth's suicide note and her aunt's suicide note. It actually impressed her so much that the essay she wrote to get into college was about this aunt's suicide, and what she had learned from that.

What Beth had learned, according to her mother, was that suicide was a legitimate alternative, and in her conversation with us, Ruth said she was sorry that she had allowed that to happen.

That's the thing, it backfired on us. I was so understanding about my sister-in-law's death—she was a schizophrenic—I ex-

104

plained it away so well that it made it legitimate for anyone to do it. Of course, once Beth had tried to kill herself the first time, I said, "Theoretically, it's okay, but not for you, and as long as you're my child, I'll do everything in my power to keep you alive." But it had become legitimized. She'd seen someone else do it. She read everything about suicide. She was obsessed with the subject.

On the morning of the day Ruth talked with us, her sister had called from California. Ruth's sixteen-year-old niece had just tried to kill herself.

Ralph is May's husband, a man in his sixties, whose father shot himself when Ralph was only three. Forty years later, Ralph's brother also killed himself.

RALPH:
My brother was a physician, a guy who was sort of "destiny's tot" in college. Second in his class in engineering, cadet colonel of the ROTC, president of the house, big man on the hill. Went on to a brilliant career in the army, decided to become a physician, moved to the West Coast. I think his medical practice had not moved as fast as he hoped it would, and I think, probably from having excessively high standards, he began to relieve some of his tensions by taking the pills that came across his desk in the routine of being a physician. That's what he said anyway. He wound up terribly addicted to all sorts of things and finally killed himself. He was not just depressed the way people get now and then. He was in a total depressed state. They had taken away his guns and he stabbed himself.

In a twist of fate that almost defies belief, May's brother also killed himself.

MAY:
I still think about him and I mourn for him. My brothers and I were very close, and I miss him. He must have been just about the same age as my father, thirty-nine or forty. He had six chil-

dren when he killed himself. He was in financial difficulty and was mixed up with another woman, just like my father. He killed himself *in the same way*—by hanging.

It was not the first or the last story in a similar vein. At the Rutgers conference we attended, a woman participant had told such a tale.

My brother committed suicide when he was thirty-nine years old. I had a grandfather who killed himself in his mid-forties. My brother was the one who found him. My brother killed himself with a gun and he was named after my grandfather. Killed himself sitting at the kitchen table.

The parallels leap out: the same kind of death, the same age, the same name.

To Sean, there is no doubt that his *father's* suicide was the cause of Frank's death.

I don't look at the other suicides or my sister's illness as an inborn thing. It's the domino theory in a way. It's very definite, as I see it: My brother Frank and my father were very close. Frank was never the same after the death. He definitely didn't have the will to live in his later years. He was making the best of it, but something inside was killing him. He was a tortured person, and he hated my mother, viciously. Their fighting was nasty and violent, caused a lot of unrest in the house. I think that affected my sister, too. You see, my brother had a very warm relationship with my father, and he blamed my mother: "You're responsible for killing Dad." It was fixed in his mind.

When he was twenty-seven, he was still fighting with my mother, blaming her. He was just crushed.

And then there was one more suicide.

My younger brother killed himself in the early morning; he had a fight with his girlfriend. Working as a bartender. Late hours. Called his best friend, said he was very troubled about his father's death, and Frank's death. Said he'd never known his father, expressed a lot of pain. Mac'd bought a shotgun weeks

106

before and blown the windows out of his house, definitely sending out signals. His friend sent over a roommate, and Mac calmed down a little; then he had another fight with his girlfriend, took his belt, and hanged himself. He was twenty-three.

Marjorie is a woman who has suffered more than her share of physical problems. She was told she would never have children because of one ailment; another left her almost paralyzed for life. She survived and had a family of three. One of the outcomes of her physical problems, though, was a conscious choice not to complain to anyone about the pain, no matter how terrible. As we listened to her survivor's story, about the suicide of her daughter—two years earlier—Marjorie made it clear that she believed her own silence played a role in the death of Rachel. What became clear was that the daughter was also a survivor, strongly affected by the suicide of two friends. As we listened to Marjorie, we realized we were being given the most complete account of a survivor's suicide that we were to get in all our conversations.

An unidentifiable foreign accent makes Marjorie's speech very exotic. Her black hair is tipped blond. She lies back in a lounge chair, grimacing from the physical pain that she only occasionally mentions.

When Rachel was very young, one day she said to me, "Mommy, how old are you?" And I said, "Take your pick; I'm the age you want me to be." "Oh, well, then, you are twenty-seven." And I thought how delightful, I don't ever have to lie. And every year she sent me a birthday card for my twenty-seventh birthday. (My birthday is exactly two weeks before hers.) Two years ago, I got a card saying, "Mommy, imagine, in a couple of weeks we will share the same age." She died on her twenty-seventh birthday.

This is not a coincidence. I don't believe in coincidences. And she told me she didn't believe in coincidences.

For ten years we knew she had suicidal tendencies; she had never tried before, but she was killing herself in working. She never stopped working, day and night. It started when she was at the high school. In her senior year, she had spent her summer at a music camp. Came back from that camp, where she had gotten very, very close to two sisters, and about a month after she came home, one of these sisters committed suicide. The girl was seventeen; it just impressed Rachel tremendously, and she talked to us about it. Then, while we could see that she was very upset, she started closing the door of her room, isolating herself (which had never happened before), but we didn't know the reason. And she didn't confide in us like she used to.

We began to go to a church that had a theater group, and they asked her to try out for a part in *Stage Door.* When they made her see that she was right for the lead, she tried out. They didn't accept her for the lead; they gave her the part of the woman who commits suicide. I did not know that. She didn't tell me. She accepted it.

And everyone came after the play and said, "Oh, wasn't Rachel incredible! She really was the best." And I felt like screaming. And then she started to think about suicide. You could have seen her doing it right there on the stage. And it was a strange thing, because until then everything in her whole life had been sunny and beautiful. She had been our sunshine, ever since she was a tiny tot. We even called her that.

Just at this time her best girlfriend said to me, "I have to talk to you. I'm concerned about Rachel." And I said I was, too. I said it all started last year when she lost a very dear friend. And she said, "Oh, Mrs. V., she didn't lose *one,* she lost *two.* Because the second sister committed suicide a month after the other." So that was when she had started closing up. At *that* point she closed the doors. That's something that's very painful to me—I feel guilty about it. She had learned how to handle her problems without talking. From me.

In college, she worked, worked, worked. She majored in Romance languages. She wrote the best thesis that they had ever read on the bachelor's degree level.

After college, she found a paralegal job. She was the number-one person. She was putting in more hours than anyone else. At one point she worked thirty-six hours without sleep. I was absolutely terrified. "Rachel you are playing with your health." I, for one, know what health is, because ever since I've been a little girl, I've had to watch it. "Oh, Mommy, don't worry, don't worry, it'll be all right." It was always she'd be "all right."

I never suspected that these problems were related to what

happened with the two sisters. Rachel looked so normal, and pretty. Except that I was aware that she was always playing a part. Especially the last years.

At first, I put all the blame of her hard work on the law firm. But it turned out that Rachel was doing this to herself. Every time there was a job no one wanted to take, she was the one who wanted to take it. Then she decided to go to law school. She almost had a breakdown the first year, because at the same time, her brother was teaching at a school, and she offered her services. She taught part-time while in law school. "Oh, Mommy, don't worry. I need that in order to accept the mentality of the people at law school." And my husband, by that time, was terrified. Please, he said, just quit. In the end, she did a beautiful job there, because everything she did was beautiful.

She accepted a full-time job at the day school. The head of the language department trained Rachel to take her place during her sabbatical. If there is one person I have a hard time to forgive—I have no bitterness, but this is the only person I feel a little anger against—it's that woman, because she used her. She had Rachel heading the language department while she was taking the year off. Of course, Rachel was terrified at the responsibility of heading the whole department and teaching French and Spanish at the same time.

The letters we received from the parents and children were so beautiful. Everyone looked at her as the dream girl—"the young lady my daughter wants to become." All the teachers were aware of the fact that she was ill, going down the drain, but none, even my son, who was extremely close to his sister, thought it was *that* bad. Our son said, "You know how she is. If she has decided to do something, no one can prevent her from doing it." And then he said, "It's the same thing as when she was a paralegal, when she was in college." And that's when I made the connection, and I became terrified. There was nothing we could do. She was really killing herself, and that was the aim. She couldn't sleep; nobody was able to help her.

All her friends and the teachers were concerned. The day before she died, three of them spoke to each other for hours and asked if there wasn't some way they could put her, by force, into a mental institution. But you know, that would have been a big mistake because she has left us with the most beautiful letters of love, and she was our friend, and now I can communicate with her spirit in peace. She is closer to me now that she's gone than she was when she was physically here, but mentally dead. And if we had put her by force into an institution, that would have meant the end of our relationship, because she would have become very angry with us, and this I could not have lived with. I could not survive with her being mad at me for hurting her.

Anyway, *I have the conviction* that she was not to survive her twenty-seventh birthday. And this keeps me from worrying and torturing myself about what "might have been." I don't go to all these meetings with parents of teenagers who are trying to see what they could have done to prevent it, because as far as I am concerned, it was bound to happen.

She cut her wrists. Strangely enough, my first thought was, "She's finally at peace, she's not suffering anymore." Later on, when I started recollecting things, I realized that I had accepted that tragedy in the same mental attitude that I had accepted my hemorrhage in the spinal cord when I couldn't walk and couldn't talk. I accepted it, and in so doing I have allowed God to help me. Because if I had rebelled and become bitter, I would have hurt myself. It is a blessing; I admit it is a blessing.

Strangely enough, although I told you that my family knows I'm not the complaining type, about six weeks before Rachel died I was talking to her on the phone. I don't know what I said, but the tone of my voice seemed to be rather down. And she said, in a very violent reaction, "Oh, I can't stand you when you feel sorry for yourself." That was a warning: You are not going to feel sorry for yourself.

We had a memorial service for her; during the ten days after her death I would wake up and hear her words. And I gathered all her thoughts, and they made my speech, and my speech came directly from this girl's mouth. I knew that too many people had too many reasons to feel guilty if they wanted to: the children who had not done their homework; her colleagues, who were very upset and knew she was getting to the end (she had lost so much weight). But she had put on a front; she had fooled absolutely everyone. Rachel was such a perfect chameleon.

110

Chapter 11

THE GRAND BARGAIN: SILENCE

Silence will not cure a disease. On the contrary, it will make it worse.
—LEO TOLSTOY

Nobody in the family wants to talk about it. You have to pretend that something terrible didn't happen.
—A SURVIVOR

When a disaster strikes, families normally are expected to talk about it: "How should we deal with this?" "How did it happen?" "Why now?" This discussion is both natural and beneficial. It allows for an expression of the pain, sorrow, anger, and frustration we feel when something terrible happens to us. Death, like any other disaster, requires a period of discussion—a time for us to express our feelings. In fact, mourning wouldn't be complete unless we had a chance to say how we felt about the person who died, unless we shed our tears and expressed our anger, our loss, our pain at his or her departure.

But it is difficult for suicide survivors to express their thoughts after a suicide. In contrast to the aftermath of "normal" deaths, friends and relatives often don't want to talk about the events surrounding a suicide. In fact, many people don't even want to admit that the death was a suicide. They hide behind a variety of myths: The death was an accident, a murder, a mystery. The reasons for this unwillingness to discuss the true nature of the death are many, but one of these is surely the fact that family members don't want to expose the blame and guilt they feel: the blame they feel toward other family members, the guilt they feel about themselves. Racked with those feelings, they cannot bare them. The silence is an attempt to keep the cap on terrible accusations—toward others and toward oneself.

In short, while most bargains are an *individual's* solution to the intense feelings after suicide, the bargain of silence is a *family's* solution to the anger and blame the members feel toward each other, and the guilt they feel about themselves. Unfortunately, it is a bargain with fearful consequences. In the last chapter, Rachel's mother briefly discussed the guilt she felt because she had taught her daughter how to "handle problems without talking." It seems to us that Marjorie is not far off the mark: Part of the cause of Rachel's suicide may have been the silence she chose after her two friends killed themselves.

Cain and Fast are eloquent on the nature of this silence and its powerful consequences; it's worth quoting them at length. As we said in chapter 9, they had been doing research with husbands and wives whose spouses had killed themselves. They point out that these were particularly disturbed people, and that they don't want to generalize about *all* survivors, but the concept of a "conspiracy of silence" that they talk about does seem familiar to many survivors.

> The shame and guilt typically brought about a massive avoidance of communication regarding the suicide, which in turn virtually prevented the *working through* of mourning. Denial, concealment, and refusal or inability to talk about the suicide tended to freeze or halt the mourning process in its earliest stages and allow minimal opportunity for it to take its normal, though disruptive course. The conspiracy of silence which tends quickly to surround a suicide sharply limits the bereaved spouse's opportunity for catharsis, for actively checking distorted fantasies against the realities of the suicidal act, for clearing up a variety of gross misconceptions, or for fully dealing with and eventually resolving the irrational guilts and particularly the angry reproaches felt towards the person who committed suicide.

This, then, is a Grand Bargain: a tacit agreement by many of the people involved *not* to discuss the suicide or the feelings evoked by the suicide. Such a silence is a remarkably effective solution to the problem of guilt and blame running rampant after suicide. It is a "gentleman's agreement" to keep the cap on those unbearable accusations. But at what a cost! And how harmful to the successful completion of the mourning process. Silence is an enemy. It compounds the impact of suicide.

On some level, most of us already know this. There is a great deal of evidence from other traumatic events in people's lives that talking about problems helps. You don't have to be a psychologist or an expert to know that's true. Leaning on a friend's shoulder, complaining, talking about your pain, crying: They all help. If I hit my thumb with a hammer, I swear, I talk about how blue it's turning, about how much it hurts. If my father dies from a heart attack, I mourn openly, discuss how much I loved him, cry on my wife's shoulder, accept accolades about him from his friends at the memorial service. But when suicides occur, many people don't talk about their feelings; there often is no memorial service and often no accolades. Indeed, there may be suspicion from the police, stares from the neighbors, disdain from the clergy, accusations from the grave, and silence from those who are too angry or guilty or afraid to talk about it. Whether it's the survivor himself who is unable to talk or his friends who are unwilling, the fact is that in many cases deadly, treacherous silence prevails.

Not that it is easy to talk about the things we feel. If you have gone through the experience, you know. One leader of a self-help group found that, even after months of working together, the group's survivors were upset when their names were printed in a newsletter. They still hadn't told their neighbors the truth about the deaths in their families. And some people won't talk about it at all.

For the family, the silence is, in fact, a solution to a serious problem. They are feeling anger at the person who died, anger at those who "didn't do enough" to prevent the suicide, guilt at their own "failings," frustration, loss, fear for the future. Remaining silent at least keeps those feelings in check, maintains an image about themselves and about their family that helps keep things on an even keel. Never mind that anger at the dead person may be appropriate—it's just too threatening.

But keeping silent just isn't a good solution; it's no answer to the

113

pain. Underneath, the feelings go on, and the result is often an inability to lead a productive life. Human bodies and human psyches express anger and guilt in other ways if the expression isn't verbal. That's what bargains are all about. And—in time—the lack of communication among family members wreaks its own havoc.

In chapter 8 we met Bernice. In further conversation, she told us how her family handled her older brother's death.

BERNICE:

He killed himself eleven years ago with an overdose of drugs, when he was eighteen. The worst part of it was the double betrayal. My parents lied to us, the three youngest children, told us it was a "lung cancer." I found out the truth from my older brothers and sisters. My parents never knew that because there was no communication. We weren't allowed to talk about him. I ended up not being able to trust anyone.

I wasn't allowed to go to the funeral, so I never got to grieve. I've spent eleven years sitting on my feelings.

In Bernice's family the results of silence seem to be a lot of disruption in both the physical and psychological lives of the children. As we said, she has Bipolar Affective Disorder and has tried to commit suicide. Her older brother is very angry. ("He wants to beat people up all the time. He drinks, goes looking for trouble.") Her sister has gastrointestinal problems and her young brother has respiratory problems. But there are other problems that continue because of the abnormal silence. After our first conversation with Bernice, she reported that her family was going to have a get-together on Saint Patrick's Day, which also happened to be the anniversary of the day her brother killed himself. It had been eleven years, but she knew that no one at the party would talk about the event. They didn't.

It was real weird. The subject of my brother's death was avoided. People looked for a way to leave early. No one talked about anything unpleasant. I also felt guilty about what I said to you. I guess I don't feel that I should talk to anyone about it at all. I'm kind of stuck on the notion that it's a disgrace. My father feels that if you talk about it, it could happen to someone else. On the one hand, you can't just put a lid on it. On the other it's impossible, with my family, to discuss it. They immediately would want to know "whose fault is it?"

So there it is, explicitly. The bargain is that if you don't talk about it, you won't have to deal with "fault." The anger and guilt won't have to come out. What a shame that Bernice's family doesn't realize how costly their bargain is.

The belief that silent healing is better than talking about things is often evident in people's conversations about the suicide in their life.

Ralph suffered from the silence surrounding his father's death, which occurred when he was three and a half. It is clear, in fact, that Ralph's entire family suffered, for, as you recall from the last chapter, his brother also killed himself, some forty years after the initial suicide. Ralph says that he was not aware of the fact that his father had killed himself until he was well into his twenties, though his two older brothers did know. But it is hard to believe that he had no inkling, considering the way children talk among themselves and the fact that adults often talk around little children as if the little ones didn't hear them. What is clear is that the rest of the family didn't want Ralph to know the truth.

> I was amazed at how badly we communicated within the family. I had asked my mother one time how my father died, quite bluntly, and she misled me into thinking that he had developed cancer and died of it.
>
> [My brothers] were seven and nine, but we never discussed the suicide. I remember when we finally did talk about it, my oldest brother said that when he was pulled out of school my uncle didn't tell him how my father had died, but when he went back to school his schoolmates said, "Nyah, nyah, your father committed suicide." That's how *he* found out.

The last comment is very revealing, because it shows one of the pernicious effects of silence: The truth usually does come out, but in a terrible fashion—in this case by way of kids who treated the suicide as something shameful.

Later, when Ralph's brother killed himself, the middle brother refused to tell his children about either his father's or his brother's suicide. According to Ralph, they simply "preferred" not to talk about it, but they, too, apparently entered into the Grand Bargain. Silence was rigidly enforced a generation later.

Sometimes, when there have been two suicides in a family, someone recognizes that silence is dangerous. Ruth, whose daughter, Beth, had taken sleeping pills, talks about her mother-in-law and the suicide of Beth's aunt, Alice.

> I think you can gain a lot from the truth, from admitting weakness. Because then you find out if there are other people out there experiencing similar difficulties or weaknesses, and when you share them, you're actually helping other people with their problems. Before Alice committed suicide, she'd been hospitalized, and my mother-in-law hid it from all her friends. Alice actually suffered from the fact that it was a hushed-up situation. It couldn't be discussed and she had to live with all sorts of stories about herself.
> My mother-in-law still thinks her friends don't know about Alice. And when Beth first attempted suicide, she told her friends that Beth had pneumonia. At the end, when Beth died, she was worried about what to tell people, and my brother and I just told her right out, angrily, "Beth committed suicide and that is the truth. Does that reflect badly on you? It does. Does it reflect badly on me? It does. That's a fact."

The fact that Ruth *could* and did talk about Beth's suicide—at length—is credited by her with her ability to keep on an even keel. She was lucky, also, to have had friends and relatives who were open to her almost endless thoughts about *why?*

> We went over and over these arguments. It's amazing to me how much we repeated ourselves and they never became impatient! They would listen and listen. And they would be willing to sit and discuss it.

But there are those who simply cannot do that. Friends, relatives, it doesn't matter. It's just too painful.

AMANDA:

I know a woman whose child died eleven years ago. The other child she sees all the time and the child does not mention it. Never. They're very close, but she will not talk about it. And I found a cousin who I hadn't seen in twenty years. She heard the story once and that was the end of that. If she thinks I'm going to cry, she says, "Oh, oh, oh." I reassure her, "I'm not going to cry. It's all right." She just doesn't want to know.

One of the more direct and painful stories about this kind of silence is that of a man whose sixty-five-year-old parents killed themselves in a suicide pact. No one would talk about the event with him—out of misplaced consideration for his feelings, out of fear, out of shame—he never knew. Then, a clergyman, an old family friend, arrived in town. Eagerly, the survivor looked forward to seeing him; at last he would get a chance to unburden himself about the suicide. But the first thing the visitor said was, "I don't want to talk about your parents' death." The man said, "But I *want* to talk about it." And the minister said, "I'm not avoiding it for your sake, I'm avoiding it for mine."

But Barbara (chapter 8) is doing it for *her* sake. And the pressure of life shows on her. She has never talked to her children about their grandfather's suicide.

I've never told them. I speak of my mother, but I still must be very angry at my father so I don't speak about him. I mean to; just this year a teacher that the two younger girls knew very well, her daughter, who was in her twenties, committed suicide. And there's been a lot of stuff on TV—they watch that and we talk about it and I've been thinking that they're getting to the point where we can talk about people and what they're like. . . . Before, I just didn't think there was any frame of reference . . . to fit it in . . . a *fact* it would flow around.

It was clear to us that Barbara's suffering, both physical and psychological, were due in part to the fact that she was not acknowledging her grief, either to herself or her children. She had not given herself the opportunity to talk about the suicide. Listen how she sounds when, during our conversation, she at last airs her feelings.

117

I feel sad, very sad. I just thought of the last time he came to visit, and he took my son for a walk, and he was there when my daughter came home from the hospital. He stayed for a month or so, and what's sad about it is that I'm sure he'd made up his mind that he was going to kill himself, because he stood on the stairway the day he left and he sang a song which he used to do when my mother was around. He would sing tiny songs to her. And he sang this song, something out of the 1920s, something popular, something about "when you think of me, think of me as 'young and gay.' " Think of me in a good way is what he was saying. And he was already gone from life, from the reality of relationships, the children; there were no holds on him—he had already drifted off. He was singing this as if he was saying it to my mother, saying good-bye. When I think of that part of him, the kind of person, then I feel sad about that, about that image, and I feel very touched by it, and I feel sad for him.

But I still make the judgment on him. I'm angry at life. It's too bad.

All of us need the openness of discussion to work through our grief. Here is Wanda talking about her need to grieve openly, how her family tried to curtail this, and how her friends and coworkers allowed it. Wanda's father, you recall, had asphyxiated himself a year earlier. Wanda was miles away at the time, and she feels guilty about not having been with him. She is also furious with him for having left her.

The thing that I did have some shame about was the intensity of my grief. That was a big issue in my family as well. I remember going home for Christmas after my father died. It had been four months. I was still in the throes, I was functioning, but I was sick. I remember my oldest brother picked me up at the airport. He came up behind me and went "Boo" and I started to cry. The whole Christmas I stayed at my brother's house, and I spent a lot of time playing the piano and reading. I felt very low-key, shut away. My brothers and sister-in-law started dumping on me because I wasn't any fun to be around. I remember my sister-in-law saying in the kitchen at my mother's house, "Gee, you're usually so much fun and you're so different this year," and I wanted to wring her neck, and I should have. I should have slapped her. I said, "I'm mourning for my father." I didn't know how else to say it. There was this pressure for me to act like it was business as usual.

My mother also wanted to shut me up prematurely about my mourning. I had a terrible fight with her over the phone, which was probably the best thing for our relationship. I told her, "I have to do this. I am sick and sad and it's not helpful for me if you try to shut me up." And then she started to tell me about her relationship with *her* mother at her father's funeral. She had started to cry and her mother went "shhh." So, her mother shut *her* up. And then my mother started to cry on the phone. It was good, it was really very good. My oldest brother couldn't deal with it at all. Everything had to be smooth, tight, set, and sealed over, and I felt like the bad one. My middle brother, when I talk to him about feeling guilty, he says something like, "What do you feel guilty about?" He has never said to me that he felt guilty, but his friends tell me that he seems weird, very self-absorbed.

I had to struggle not to be a good girl, I had to struggle not to be afraid to disrupt other people with my upset. It was the hardest thing to do. And I think it was because my father's death was so important to me that I was able to do it. I mean, I find that there are some things that are so important to me that I don't give a shit who I upset. But it was hard not to say, "I'm okay." I talked with a client who felt guilty about being so upset and angry about a suicide in her family, and I said, "Please, this is the one chance in your life that you can really fall apart, so don't miss it," and I really presented it as an opportunity for her to look deep inside herself.

To sum up, the bargain of silence is a solution to one kind of problem, but creates others. We have suggested that it's a grand bargain, an umbrella over many of the other bargains, providing a shelter under which they can safely operate. We have said that many of the survivor's physical and psychological problems *derive* from that silence, that the effects of suicide that we have discussed throughout this book owe their power, if not their existence, *to* silence.

Were *we* responsible for the suicide? Was it really suicide? How, actually, did they kill themselves? If, through our inability or unwillingness to talk, we do not get a chance to experience those feelings and to compare our fantasies with reality, relief simply does not occur.

Psychoanalysts call the transformation of experience in therapy "working through," and something like it can occur in everyday life. Each time you talk about a painful experience there is a little change. It's almost as if experience is like a kaleidoscope: Each turn permits the elements to realign themselves. If the turn is allowed there's some reorganization, some give, things feel a little better. There are tiny transformations. You are able to shift into a more comfortable mode, so that you feel less despairing about the same reality.

Silence freezes mourning. The longer we resist talking to those who are closest to us, the harder it is to unfreeze it. No matter how deeply our feelings are buried, we eventually suffer the consequences.

There may be other reasons why people maintain the conspiracy of silence. Among them is the sad belief that they somehow ally themselves with the dead person by staying silent. It is one way of uniting themselves with the loved one, who, after all, is also silent.

Another reason people may remain silent is that they realize the impossibility of communicating with the one person they really want to talk to—the person who killed himself. This sense of having a conversation *cut off* in the middle is very strong after a suicide has occurred. The person who dies has had the last word, and there is *nothing* we can do about it. No wonder we don't want to talk. Nothing anyone can say will change the fact of our loved one's death, and nothing we can say will get to the person we love the message we may feel we never said, or at least never said strongly enough: "Don't go, I love you."

Bargains are a survivor's friend and a survivor's enemy. Each provides an escape from painful, disruptive anger, but each leads the survivor down the path to a thorn bed of problems. As future chapters will make clear, we believe that the primary road to dealing with *all* of a survivor's problems is to lift the silence. Silence is indeed the enemy. Relief from confusion, depression, anger, and guilt lies in ending it, in learning how to talk about the suicide.

Chapter 12

REACTIONS TO
AN ADOLESCENT'S SUICIDE

For the surviving parent, the suicide of an adolescent son or daughter is a terrible tragedy. In the story that follows can be seen the fears, the anger, the guilt, the pain, the bargains, and the continuing grief that pursue so many survivors and, especially, parents of young suicides. But Elizabeth's story is also a transition to the third section of this book, which deals with coping. Her son, Charles, killed himself almost four and a half years ago, and she is now beginning to see the future in a somewhat different light than in the preceding period. Despite her grief, her bargains, and her guilt, Elizabeth is coming to terms with her son's suicide.

Elizabeth's voice makes her sound much older than she is; you could close your eyes and imagine a woman in her sixties. She is eager to speak, but there is a tension in her voice. Her words tumble out one after the other. She has put on a lot of weight since the suicide.

In 1974, we moved into this house. We had two children of our own (a boy and a girl). The next year was the collapse of Vietnam, and we adopted some Vietnamese children. First Fred, then came Charles and Joan—they're brother and sister. Their mother had died the year before, and their father allowed us to adopt them. He lives in the U.S., and Charles and Joan saw him a good deal. [All Elizabeth's adopted children call Charles and Joan's real father Papa; Elizabeth and her husband are called Mom and Dad.] Then came Larry. Charles died four years ago this past April sixteenth. That was before the so-called teen suicide epidemic. He was with us seven years.

My only other experience with suicide was my next-door neighbor when I was a child. I was about fourteen. I was the last person to see this man alive. I remember I had to go out with the police searching for him, and they did find him. He had jumped into a clay pit. And then his son committed suicide, years later.

What Happened

I'm an operating-room nurse. I was operated on myself a couple of times some years ago, and afterward I decided I wanted to be a nurse, and I told my surgeon, Dr. R., and he became kind of my mentor. I was thirty-eight.

It just so happened I was working at the hospital when I got the telephone call from the police about Charles. I turned to the unit head and I said, "Get Dr. R." In those few seconds I remember my legs buckling from under me, but I had the presence of mind to turn over the narcotic keys. I left the floor and went down to the nurse's room, and I said, "My son is dead" (I just had that feeling he was already dead), and I wondered why they were all standing around. I said, "Why aren't you doing something?" But they hadn't even brought him into the hospital yet.

Charles had driven the car into the garage, closed the door, and hooked up the exhaust. Fred happened to come home early from school that day—he skipped a class—and he found the body. He turned off the ignition, he opened the garage door, he tried to start Charles breathing again. He did everything a person could, without being overcome himself. And he called for help.

The first thing they wanted to do was shoot me full of Valium, but I wasn't hysterical. I said get Dr. R.; the head nurse down there knew I was his patient and that I was one of his favorites.

122

Strangely, he had just come into the hospital, and she reached him. He broke down and cried, but then he composed himself before he came over to me. He said something to me that has carried me—I think it's kept me alive. I remember saying, "Tom, why, why, why?" And "How can I tell his real father?" Tom said, "You must tell his father." And I said, "Why did he do this? He just got an eleven-thousand-dollar scholarship to Princeton, and a scholarship to another college." And Tom said, "Elizabeth, I'd like to feel he had a scholarship with you." What a beautiful thing to say.

This doctor is a sensitive, beautiful human being. For months, he would call me every night to see how I was.

Reactions

I never stop asking why. But I think everyone's reaction in the family was a little different. About a year ago, the third anniversary, I was very down, and I remember my husband yelling, "I hate Charles." I couldn't believe he could say that. And he said, "Charlie took my wife away." And then I realized what had happened, that I couldn't be as open as I had; I had to hide some emotions.

The night he died, I asked two friends to come by. One woman had lost a child in an accident, the other knew how I felt. I wanted *them* there, not that priest who didn't know how I felt. My friend said to me, "What a terrible thing for Charlie to do to you." I couldn't understand at the time what she meant, but now I know.

But *I've* never gotten angry and I feel that's maybe why I haven't healed. Fred got angry that first night, went upstairs, tearing apart Charlie's room. "Why did he do this? Why did he do this to Papa? Why did he do this to Mom and Dad? Why, why, why?"

Charlie was a very unusual child, he was probably the one closest to me. Everyone tries to make the picture rosy after someone's died, but I'm not exaggerating. I never had to discipline him. With the other kids, I used to say, "Am I destined to hear rock and roll the rest of my life?" But this child played the piano—it was Mozart and Beethoven—everything a mother dreams of. This was a child you never had to tell, "Go study." He was kind of your dream son. Of course, the other kids have other things that are very special about them, but Charlie was different.

Guilt

I graduated first in my class in nursing school. I was thirty-eight years old. It took a lot out of me and it took a lot out of the family. All the times I spent out of the house. All the blame. I kept thinking, if, if, if . . . If I hadn't been away so much. If I hadn't asked him to iron my uniform the night before. (All the kids have jobs. Charlie loved to iron. He was a terrific ironer.) I've taken it so personally, and yet I know he loved me. I know that.

I was known in town as Super Mother. Not only did I adopt four kids, but I had dozens of other kids from all over the world live with us at different times.

I went to a psychiatrist right after Charlie died, and that man almost killed me. If I'd have had an older car, I think I would have driven it right off the bridge. He said, "You weren't enough." No mother needs to hear she wasn't enough. There I was paying him seventy-five dollars to fall asleep while I was talking to him. And telling me I wasn't enough! I didn't need that. I think I was smart enough to get myself out of his grips, because he would have destroyed me. Of course I wasn't enough to keep Charlie alive. No one was. But say it that way; don't say, "You weren't enough."

What did I feel? *That good mothers' children don't commit suicide.*

Charlie's real father was so good to us. He gave us his most precious gift. And I caused him that pain. I wish I could get over that feeling.

I have a mother who's never been able to say it's her fault. About anything. I think it's a soul-cleansing thing to say it's my fault. I do it in the operating room. "I forgot." Or "I didn't feel like doing it." I've tried to make a point of always accepting responsibility when I'm wrong.

It certainly wasn't lack of love on my part, I can tell you that. I remember when I came out of the psychiatrist's office the second time, I shouted, "You think we didn't love you? You think we didn't love you? Well, look at us now, if you're anywhere where you're looking down on us." And there's a part of me that knows he *had* to know we loved him. But it's not a matter of love, is it? Love just isn't enough . . .

My husband said, after a few years, that he'd thought about it and thought about it, and there was nothing he could have done to prevent Charlie's death. He was going to go on with his life.

Charlie had a great sense of humor; he always had the last line. And this time he *did* have the last line. The child who gave me no pain in his lifetime has given me the most pain. That pain will never go away. Oh, maybe it's eased up a little. I can maybe go fifteen minutes now without thinking about it. God, that is progress! That *is* progress.

Neighbors and Friends

People say the craziest things to you. I withdrew from people, and I lost a lot of friends. I have one close friend a couple of streets away who has remained a good friend. But there are a lot of people who can't come talk to me. Can't handle it. One neighbor was here when they were trying to resuscitate Charlie, and every time I saw her afterward, she turned her head. I went down to the school a couple of months later. She couldn't look at me.

I was on the street one time, and someone came right out and said, "Did Charlie kill himself because he didn't get into Harvard?" I said, "Charlie didn't apply to Harvard. He didn't want to go to Harvard."

Then there was another person I met on the street. Someone said I shouldn't have answered her, but I did. She said, "Did Charlie kill himself because he was homosexual?" I said, "I don't know whether Charlie was a homosexual or not, and if he was, whether he knew it or not. I'll tell you what: I'd rather have a homosexual son alive than a dead heterosexual one." And I truly feel that. I thought, how stupid! It was a shock that someone would say that.

125

I guess people need answers.

There was a realtor down the block who talked about our house to people he showed around, and he'd say, "That's the suicide house." But my husband had an answer for that: He said our house has seen so many good times it can take some tragedies too.

We had a private funeral service because Charlie's father was Buddhist, and there were certain things that had to be done. It was very important for him to say certain prayers as soon as he could, so my husband and he and I went down to the funeral home and we were put in the basement, and he was saying his prayers, and my husband was standing beside him sobbing through the whole thing, an hour and a half of standing while those prayers were said, and workmen were down there banging around, and they were looking at us. It was a horrible thing to have to go through. Then we went up and he was cremated in front of us. None of the other kids were involved. But we had a service the next day, Sunday, here, and I invited his friends and the real close friends of ours. I always thought that was the most sane way to have a funeral. I don't like funeral homes and never have, that filing past the casket and that saying, "I'm sorry." People are glad it didn't happen to them is what they're almost saying.

Fears

It was a year before I let myself go into the garage. Then I did it like a dare. Exactly a year after he died.

There is always that fear of something else happening. We were all together Christmas Day. Then Larry left at ten-fifteen to go be with his girlfriend. (She was having some problems.) After a while, we all asked, "Where's Larry?" No one knew. You know what it took to go out—thinking that something had happened to him—to go in the garage with a flashlight, looking for him, thinking that he might be *hanging?* It was a sleeting, snowy night. I called his girlfriend's house at one-fifteen. And I thought, well, maybe I'm going to disturb her mother, but she'll understand. And the girl answered right away and said, "Oh, no, he's not here." I said, "If you see him, send him on home." Then I turned out all the lights and laid down in the den. And I looked at that clock. I said at two-thirty I'll call the police. At two-twenty-nine he came in the door. I said, "Where've you been?" "Oh, Sharon needed me, I had to go to her." I said, "If you'd told me, I would have driven you down there." We were up until four o'clock in the morning, with me telling him what he'd put me through. "Don't you see that you're loved? Why do you have to do this to me?" I tried to show him how cruel that was to do that to somebody.

Fred is twenty. He wanted to learn how to fly. I wrote him a note and said, "Don't." He went anyway. I said to my husband, "If he dies, I am not going to his funeral. I'm going on vacation. And it's going to be an embarrassment to all of you!" And then Fred said, "You can't let your fears go on." I said, "I buried one son and that's enough. I'm not burying any more of you. I'm not going to do it. That's enough."

Bargains

After Charles died, I wanted to die. One hot summer night I had come home from work and I'd poured a glass of iced tea, and no one was home. I had a Danish girl staying here, and she had put the knives *up* in the drainboard, and I had always trained the kids you put them down. I reached over and ripped open my arm, and it was bleeding. This was just a few months after Charles's death, maybe June or July, and I couldn't stop it, and here I am an operating-room nurse, and I said, "So what, if I die? It's fine." I just watched it bleed. I didn't care. I've seen people ex-sanguinate, it's not so bad. And then I said, "No, I *don't* want to die," and I put point pressure and a tourniquet, and it was fine.

I remember right after Charlie died, my favorite niece was being married in Florida. I hated to fly but I did fly to see her, and I said, "I don't care. If I die, I get to see Charlie. And if I don't die, that's okay, too."

I think I became a robot. I worked extra hard and asked for extra time, and worked weekends because I couldn't face coming home, especially in the afternoons, which was the time I

127

spent with Charlie. That's when I got overtired and had to get some help. You don't realize what you're doing to yourself.

Like eating. I've gained eighty pounds since Charlie died. I'm trying to work on that now, because there's pain in being fat too. But you know, I figured that that's a form of suicide. Overeating isn't good for you. Certainly not this kind of weight. But it's like I had to punish myself. Some people may starve themselves; I went the other way.

Silence

I wish that sometime my husband would initiate the talk. If he has some little memories—just to reach out. He's a very tender, loving man, but there's just that one spot that's missing. If he could just squeeze my hand and say, "This reminds me of Charlie." I think, in the beginning, you spare each other because you think, "Is he really thinking the same thing I'm thinking?" and if he's not, you don't want him to have the pain you're having. If he's gotten by this little memory, this song or something that sets it off, if he's spared that, I don't want to hurt him by bringing it up. The same with the kids.

I don't know how the other kids feel anymore. We don't talk about it. Do they feel guilty? I hope not. Fred did everything he could to save Charles. So did the police. But I really don't know how they feel. There's something about talking about it that makes everyone uncomfortable.

Mourning and Grieving

I've found a knitting store in town, and it's like my pub. People who've taken me as I was and allowed me to be just me. A complete change from my job.

I still have my down moments. I'm on call for emergencies one night a month. The night of Memorial Day weekend the phone rang. Dinner was on the table, and there I was, dashing off to the hospital. There was a young man who had shot himself. And we also had someone with a perforated ulcer. Then, when

128

I was ready to go home, there was a call about a boy who had hung himself. I had to go down to the emergency room, and we opened his chest. Two suicides in one night. It was in the same room where they brought my son. The girls in the E.R. aren't used to opening chests, so they were delighted I was there and knew what the hell I was doing. The surgeon walked in. He's a very insensitive man, and he said, nastylike, "Whatever would possess someone to do this to himself?" And I thought that was an awful thing for him to say with me standing there.

There's a part of me that doesn't want to be over it. I mean you want to be over it, but you don't want to forget those seven years. I don't want to forget that child. His natural sister came down and asked, "In all your pain, would you rather not have had him?" And I said, "No!"

You see, it's almost like saying, "I don't want to let go of you. I don't want you to go way in the back of my mind like my Spanish is in the back of my mind."

My husband always says that he married me because I was strong. His mother was strong, his sister was strong, I'm strong. If anyone was going to survive, it was me. But I don't want to be known as a rock. I want to be known as a weakling.

My life has not been conventional. When I went to nursing school at thirty-eight, my father (he'll be eighty next month) said, *"Now* what're you doing?" When I got a new child, *"Now* what're you doing? Who's living in your house now?" When Charlie died, my mother came down here with my sister and her husband. My father wasn't up to it. He's never said to me, "Betty, I'm sorry." I guess I've been searching for a father. I think every daughter always wants that person to put his arms around her—not a husband image, but a father image—and say, "I'm sorry." The closest I've had is this particular doctor. There's a spark there. Something special.

I've just started working part-time, three days a week, because I realize there's no point in killing myself. It's very demanding work. Not only physically but mentally. And I enjoy being home again. To cook and enjoy other things and to go out to lunch once in a while. And have a little levity. And that just happened. But I feel guilty about it. I *shouldn't* enjoy things. I don't deserve to enjoy.

Because *good mothers' kids don't commit suicide.*

Getting Help and Giving It

My son-in-law's parents said to me, "This is the worst day in your life. No day will ever be worse than this." And it's true. No matter what happens, it can't be worse than that. It's been my own war zone.

I had pastoral counseling for a year and a half. I was working so hard, and one day in the operating room Dr. R. saw that I was "losing it." He said I *had* to call the counselor. And I did, thank God.

And then there was the group I went to, with other survivors.

I guess there's a bonding of those of us who've been through it. With that boy who killed himself that night—Memorial Day—there was so much that I wanted to reach out and say to his parents.

I don't feel my mission is over yet. There's something that has to be done. I think those of us that have been through it have much to offer to those just going through it. Because there's such isolation. And if I hadn't made that phone call (to the self-help group) and if I hadn't had a supervisor in the O.R. who saw me going down for the third time—I mean, those people saved me.

By "mission" I mean I want to be part of something. Like the people who go around after someone's had a mastectomy. Or the cancer support teams. To help people who've been through this.

I want to share something with you. Yesterday I went into the hospital, and there were three cases. The last one I dreaded. It was a little girl, five years old. Two years ago I'd been in the O.R. when we operated on her for cancer. She'd had chemotherapy and now she was coming back. They'd found a mass in her abdomen. I can tell you I didn't want to be there, but it was my job. She was crying and fighting. She didn't want to go into the O.R. She asked for her mother, and I tried to talk to her and

130

explain what was going to happen, and she wanted to know why she had to have an operation and were we going to give her needles and hurt her, and it was awful. Then the surgeon opened her up, and he saw that she only had a cyst, and it was benign. And he sent me out into the waiting room to tell her father and mother. They stood up when they saw me coming and I could see what they were expecting. I said, "It's okay. It's only a cyst. And it's benign." They didn't believe me. "Are you telling us the truth? That's *all?*" I nodded. And they said, "Are you sure?" And I said, "Yes, I'm sure."

That kind of day gives me strength to go on.

Part Three

GIVING HELP AND GETTING HELP
Listening and Talking

Chapter 13

RESPONDING

I want to feel good about myself again.
—A SURVIVOR

The first two sections of this book have been about some of the reactions survivors have to the suicides in their lives. This section is about *responding*.

Instead of being passive victims of their fate, survivors can make accommodations and can respond to fate; they can become active in their own behalf and active in their own lives. So, when we say responding, we are talking about the use of as many parts of the survivor's being as possible, about becoming unstuck, about continuing a process in which the survivor is a participant, not an observer. Responding, not reacting.

How does a survivor do this? How does he see to it that he doesn't get trapped—in silence, in unproductive bargains? We will try to talk, as much as possible, in specifics, about what we think it would be helpful to know about how people work themselves out of such situations. What has been shown to help. What has been shown to be unproductive.

It may help to know that most survivors feel depressed or helpless or angry. They feel lonely, unloved, abandoned. The anger turns inward, and they have thoughts of suicide themselves. But it may also help to know that these feelings, with their sense of "I cannot go on like this," need not be permanent. It is possible to change. Others have done it.

RESPONDING

1. Responding is not the same as forgetting about what happened. It does not mean that you can expect to get over the suicide completely. But it *is* thinking good thoughts about the dead person; it is learning not to feel responsible for the suicide; and it's the ability to feel good about yourself again.

2. Responding takes time; all survivors discover that. During that time many of the feelings of despair, depression, anger, and guilt may continue. But you should know that many survivors seek a variety of forms of professional and nonprofessional help and as a result manage to feel better sooner. One thing is clear: in seeking help, earlier is better than later.

3. It is normal to experience these painful feelings, and helpful to express them. Suicidal thoughts, for instance, are natural as a response to the suicide of someone close to you. Anger is natural. Relief that "it's over" is natural. Some guilt is natural. Fear is natural. Loss of self-esteem is natural. Depression is natural. You should not feel that you are "losing it" if you acknowledge these feelings, and you should by now realize that many many others have also shared these feelings.

4. Mourning is essential. We mean by mourning something that allows you to take time out from the real world to think about the dead person and your relationship with him or her. During the mourning period, no matter how brief, your focus is on the dead person. Perhaps you will ask questions about him and about your place in the world; you may be totally preoccupied with his or her death. But you will also return to your normal life having made an *adjustment* to that death, able to respond to the world around you. Mourning is necessary. But many survivors don't get an opportunity to mourn because they are stuck. Their real feelings are so distanced, their guilt so great, their anger so intense, that they stay in their grief, repeating their litany, not moving ahead. For such people, some form of outside help is necessary.

SORTING OUT YOUR FEELINGS

Throughout this book we have discussed a range of feelings that survivors generally have after a suicide. It might help to go back over them from the vantage point of responding—of where we might expect these feelings to move.

Guilt

As a survivor, you may feel guilt, a guilt that comes from your anger *before* the death, your anger *at* the death, a sense of helplessness, ambivalence about the dead person, even a finger pointing from the grave, saying, "You did this to me."

You will probably need to feel guilty for a while, but it might help you to know that many survivors eventually come to accept the fact that they are *not* responsible for the death of their loved one. Or, short of that, that there are limits on how responsible they have to feel.

Anger

Some people describe this as rage, others as hostility. It may be anger at the dead person for abandoning you or for accusing you; it may be anger at someone else, someone who you feel is responsible for the death; or it may be anger at yourself.

This, too, may continue for a long time. Some survivors find that the anger changes in focus and intensity as time goes on. Others find relief when they can express the anger they feel toward the dead person.

Helplessness and Fear

These feelings are generally at their worst right at the beginning, but fears can come back to haunt you at any time. Will another person in my life abandon me in the same fashion? Will I kill myself? Can I ever go back to my routine? Will I feel safe again?

Generally, survivors find that as they continue with their lives, as people do *not* abandon them or die or commit suicide, the fears diminish. They are able to respond more and more fully to the world around them.

Depression

The most pervasive feeling for all people suffering from trauma is depression. It may help you to know that anger that remains *unexpressed* is very often the cause of depression. (The anger turns in on oneself.) Some people find that recognizing whom they are really angry at relieves the depression. In chapter 17 a number of survivors tell stories about their attempts to respond; it's interesting that there's something about helping other people that specifically makes some of them feel good and seems to help dispel their depression.

Loss

Loss is difficult. People are irreplaceable. You have loved someone and that loved one is gone. That loss will not go away, nor can you expect it to. How important a role the sense of loss plays in your life is another matter. You can remember, and have positive feelings for, the dead person without continuing to grieve.

THINGS THAT MAKE RESPONDING
MORE DIFFICULT

It might help you to know what some people have found gets in the way of learning to respond.

Silence

Time and again in our conversations with survivors we heard how the natural propensity to talk (humans are normally communicative animals) was curtailed. And it's amazing how many times the wish not to talk was hidden behind old bromides: "Why not let sleeping dogs lie?" "Don't open old wounds." "I'm all right, I don't need to talk." "My husband and I can deal with this by ourselves." "It won't help to dwell on it." Or this statement, by the father of one young man who had killed himself: "If you talk about it, everyone will get upset and then someone else will kill themselves."

In retrospect, most survivors feel that all of this is simply a cover for the inability to talk about the suicide. And that, as we have said, is a dangerous thing.

Ambivalence

Prolonged grief among suicide survivors is not always what it appears to be—that they've lost somebody whom they've loved too much. Long before the suicide, that loving was also tinged with anger, because *all* relationships—even loving ones—also involve angry feelings toward each other. What often makes things difficult in mourning is the suppressed anger, especially if there is a lot of it. In those relationships where there has been relatively little anger, the mourning can be cleaner, quicker, and more complete. Protracted mourning is typical of intensely ambivalent relationships, that is, ones in which there is much, as yet unresolved, anger.

Parents

The guilt and depression among parental survivors *does* seem to be more intense and longer lasting than among others. Every single parent to whom we talked expressed this same feeling: Their "job" had been to protect their child—and they had failed. Perhaps their worst nightmare of this is the fear that if one child dies by suicide, others will too. Parents sometimes express intense anger toward their dead

139

child, followed by denial of those feelings, then intense guilt and depression.

What can anyone say about this devastating experience? As parents ourselves, we know that parents feel particularly responsible for the behavior and safety of their children. But many parents come to see that they can never control their children's lives; that from an early age children begin to exercise some control over themselves—and we, as parents, encourage them to do so. (If they did not, children could not grow up into adulthood.) The plain fact is that parents are not so powerful that they can keep their children from making mistakes, even the tragic mistake of suicide. A clear expression of this came from the father of one young man who had killed himself.

> I'll answer your question. You can't do a thousand and one
> things bringing up a child. You can only do a thousand. Each
> parent does the best he can. More than that he can't do.

In the final analysis, responding probably requires that survivors accept the fact that they could not and cannot govern everything that happens. This is not a simple matter; if it were, parental survivors would not suffer as much as they do. But it can allow them to give up some of their crippling guilt.

Men

Compared with women, men are particularly bad at finding their place during the mourning period. They are very good, however, at saying, "I don't need to talk." In 1985 the *Journal of Hospital and Community Psychiatry* reported on a National Academy of Sciences study that showed that "bereaved" men were at much higher risk than women. Women seem to deal better with death. Men who have lost a spouse or parents show a significant increase in death from heart disease, infectious illness, and accidents. Add to that a Johns Hopkins University study that showed that their reluctance to express emotions keeps many widowers from seeking the help they need to cope with grief—which in turn results in a high rate of depression, alcoholism, and other disturbances—and one can see why male suicide survivors are a high-risk group.

Few men join self-help groups, and even when they do join them, they seldom participate the way women do. Women seem to express their grief and anger and explain their feelings more easily. Men tend to sit there listening. Apparently, they have a harder time expressing their feelings, so a lot more pain stays inside them. In actual fact, the "I'm all right, I don't need to talk" approach is often *not* a sign that a man is doing fine, but a cover-up for his inability to express painful feelings.

OTHER THINGS THAT MAKE RESPONDING MORE DIFFICULT

- *Blame and scapegoating.* One survivor said, "A family has to come to see that nobody is to blame."
- *Not having a support system.* Friends, relatives, a job, other people to support you.
- *Blaming the suicide for all life's problems.* It is likely that the suicide is only one piece of a troubled life. Things went wrong before the suicide and are likely to go wrong afterward. A survivor has to try to be realistic about that fact.
- *Endless rescue fantasies.* "If only I'd done this, if only I'd done that."
- *Discovering the body.* Those survivors who have been unfortunate enough to actually find the body of the suicide can expect their trauma to be greater. This is fact.
- *Thinking that an end to grief is the same thing as forgetting the loved one.* Some people think that if they stop grieving, that's the same as forgetting (or giving up) the dead person. It just isn't true. Survivors can express their love for the loved one in many ways, but holding on to grief needn't be one of them. There are some people who feel they need the person they have lost in order to keep on with their lives. They feel that their own personal survival is actually threatened as a consequence of the suicide. In a very real sense, these survivors feel the dead person was a *part* of them. For such survivors, professional help

141

may be the only way to move on through the normal mourning process.

WHAT *HELPS* PEOPLE TO RESPOND

Doing Something

You should know that *doing something* is helpful. Anyone who suffers from periods of depression knows what a wonderful relief it can be to get up in the morning and *do* something, because depression—that inward-turning anger—responds very well to action. Unfortunately, many survivors are incapacitated by their grief and cannot *do*.

Early on in the grieving period, however, there is at least one thing all survivors *can* do that many find to be helpful. They can involve themselves in the normal rituals: a memorial service, a funeral, an announcement in the paper. Many survivors told us that this did *not* occur and that that contributed to the family's agony.

RALPH:

My brother's family didn't want a "party," so they decided to have nothing at all. We just went home.

A WIFE:

We didn't have a memorial service; we moved. There was no external sign of Sam's suicide. It was a mistake.

Human beings generally make ceremonies of big moments. We work hard at marking them as a way of underlining their meaning. Public and private ceremonies allow us to see what things mean to us. Our Fourth of July celebration is a large-scale example, as are religious and cultural holidays.

But smaller events are also marked: birth (we send out announcements, call our relatives and friends, accept presents) and marriage (a party, friends, a honeymoon), and puberty rites ("sweet sixteen" parties). Deaths, in particular, are almost always marked (wakes, sitting shiva, funerals, memorial services, lighting candles on the anniversary, black wreaths, and so on).

Sometimes we are not so clear about our feelings about these events. The ceremony is a way of defining what things mean and of reinforcing that meaning. And that's useful because when meanings are made clear, we are always more comfortable. Sometimes we don't know how we really feel until we participate in such an activity. Funerals or memorial services help many people define how they feel about the dead person.

But, as we have seen, many survivors avoid any formal marking of the death. By not holding a memorial service or even a funeral, they deprive themselves of an early opportunity to mourn and to mark what was valuable in the life that has been lost.

Of course it's important to find the kind of ceremonies and rituals that are meaningful to *the survivor.* Someone else's may have limited value, but whatever ceremony is chosen—big or small, public or private, conventional or innovative—it can be a kind of punctuation mark, an ending and a beginning, a way to help the survivor to move on to the next emotional step. In years to come, a repetition of the marking (an anniversary) can allow us to see how far we have come and how far there is to go in learning to respond.

Finding Support

John McIntosh, a psychologist at the University of Indiana, suggests that there are "wizards of coping," people who "send out signals" and, consequently, get all sorts of help in learning to respond. Some people send out no signals and get no support.

When tragedy strikes, being alone can make the tragedy much more painful. It helps if the suicide survivor can establish contact with other human beings who can help the survivor conquer some of that sense of loneliness. People who do better in responding are those whose environment (people and institutions) provides a chance for the survivor to feel safe, connected, part of the world. Survivors can help themselves by *searching out* such an environment, by not allowing themselves to fall back into loneliness and sorrow. There are people who will care—we need to seek them out.

Talking

It will come as no surprise that we feel that the most important way to learn to respond to a suicide is through talking. Keeping silent, hiding your feelings about the suicide, punishing yourself, only perpetuates the grief. *Expressing* grief and pain, anger and guilt, is healthy. Finding someone who will listen is a major part of being able to talk. Our next three chapters deal with talking and listening, learning to find someone to talk to and learning how to talk about suicide.

In chapter 14 ("Giving Help by Listening") we start by defining the whole notion of what help for survivors is all about and we suggest ways for would-be helpers to give it. Then, in chapter 15 ("Getting Help by Talking"), we move on to ways that survivors can *get* help. Chapter 16 concerns itself with the painful problem of children who have lost a parent to suicide. Finally, some stories about those who are already learning to respond (chapter 17, "Living with Suicide.")

At the beginning of this chapter we said that learning to respond with more and more of yourself takes time. We should add that some feelings may never go away: some sense of loss, the need to find an "explanation." You will have memories, some sweet, some sad. And why shouldn't you? Someone who was an important part of your life has died. There's no reason for you to forget them. What we can hope is that, increasingly, the memories will be pleasant ones, not continually bringing with them anger, guilt, and depression.

You cannot ever undo the suicide, nor even make it less tragic, but as a result of responding to it you can go on about your life in a way that's healthier, more creative, more productive; with the proper philosophical distance and balance; not needing to deny that what is sad is sad, but seeing things for what they are; not having to block or limit or cut off aspects of yourself.

This often means giving up or changing a bargain. Because bargains are habits, and habits are hard to give up or change, you'll need some help in doing this. And that's what this next section of the book is all about.

Chapter 14

GIVING HELP BY LISTENING

He was great because he just let me cry and carry on and he didn't try to "fix it," he didn't try to make it better. I told him that since he had no pat answer and no smooth solution—he just listened—it was marvelous!

—WANDA

When a friend or neighbor *wants* to be of some comfort, he often finds himself standing by helplessly, not quite knowing what to do or say. The survivor often does not send a clear signal about what he or she wants from friends and loved ones. Does she want to talk or to be left alone? Does he want to express his anger or bury it? Often, in fact, the survivor himself doesn't know. And the would-be helper is confused or embarrassed or inhibited—drawn unwittingly into the grand bargain of silence. Or, if talk is going on, it often is talk that *obscures* the true feelings and denies the true meaning of the suicide.

If friends were clearer that there was something they could do, and if they knew what that something was, they would probably be less likely to be paralyzed at precisely the moment they are most needed. Our aim in this chapter is to make clear what can be done and to offer some suggestions about how to be helpful to a suicide survivor. The chapter is based on some ideas about what psychological help is all about: that what helps most is to create a climate in which a person's own capacity to heal himself can flourish. That climate is one in which the helper mainly *listens*.

This is true not only for suicide survivors but for all people who need help.

GOALS IN HELPING

To begin with, the goals of both helper and person in need have to be properly defined.

Nothing will bring back a lost loved one. Nothing will undo what has been done or erase what has been said in so final an act as suicide. But what cannot be cured or changed *can* be borne more easily.

The goal in providing help for people, then, has to do with *bearing loss, pain, and personal tragedy more easily.* Helping suicide survivors means finding a way for them to be less stuck in tragedy and more able to go on with the business of life. Help means finding a way for survivors to make bargains that are less costly. It means getting survivors to respond better. It means cutting through the terribly costly silence.

Guidelines for Helping

As a helper, what do you need to know?

Mental health professionals have studied this question exhaustively. Some of what has been discovered is very encouraging: Ordinary people can help each other. Of course, some expertise and training as a helper can be especially valuable (particularly where people's reactions are extreme), but there are many things that a nonexpert, nonprofessional can do that make an enormous difference. In fact, it's important for us to stress that you do not have to be an expert. You do have to be eager to help and, above all, be willing to listen to someone who is in trouble and in pain. This is at the core of what a good psychotherapist does, and it is what ordinary people can do for each other, too.

- You need to know that as a helper you do not have to fix things up for people.

In other words, you don't have to have *the* answer. In fact, it isn't even particularly helpful to offer answers. Statements like "Perhaps it's

146

better this way" or "Be brave for the children's sake" or "Cry it out" or "Don't cry" have a way of sounding tinny, flat, and irrelevant. And they tend to *be* irrelevant. Survivors need help in working out their own answers. Ultimately, it is *their* answers that are the only ones that are not irrelevant.

- You need to know that a person's own experience of what things mean is self-corrective if it is allowed to be.

The meaning of things changes. A suicide that is experienced at first as an accusation can come to be seen (for example) as the outcome—albeit, sad outcome—of an illness that nobody could do anything about. This is a change in meaning and an important one. There is much less guilt and much less pain in seeing things this way.

Change normally tends to occur in a self-corrective direction; that is, given the chance, in the right emotional climate, the meaning of things gets better, not worse. Good help provides that chance. It gives survivors the opportunity to come to their own, productive answers.

- You need to know that good listening permits good talking.

The right kind of talking can be enormously helpful. It is helpful precisely because it allows people to focus on what things mean to them, *and then to refocus.* This focusing and refocusing, in an atmosphere of safety, is what produces change. Talking is the process by which most people figure out what things mean to them and then figure out what things could mean.

Offering to listen is the best way to offer help to someone who needs to talk.

- There are some rules for listening well.

New information, new perspectives, new insights change the meaning of things, but not just new information, perspectives, and insights gathered from outside sources. New knowledge from within also changes the meaning of things.

Good listening aims at helping people to focus on what they already know, but don't necessarily *know* they know. Information that is inside may be frightening or difficult to acknowledge. Good listening aims at making it safe to acknowledge what is already known.

Below we offer some suggestions for how to listen well. In doing this, we have taken inspiration from psychologist Eugene Gendlin's book, *Focusing*—a wonderful book with much to say about good listening.

SOME RULES FOR GOOD LISTENING

Rule 1. The first goal is to establish a listening attitude.

To listen to someone requires a genuine eagerness to hear what that person is saying and is going to say. It involves respecting his or her way of thinking and organizing thoughts. It requires genuine curiosity—a feeling that is free of presuppositions about what someone should or must feel and an eagerness to know what it is that he or she *is* thinking and feeling.

This attitude is easier to describe than to establish because it requires that the listener let go of his or her own way of thinking and defining things. This kind of letting go is especially difficult when we are hearing about disturbing or painful experiences. What often happens then is that we want to define things in our own way.

Think, for example, of someone coming to you with the painful, perhaps shameful, feelings he has about the suicide of his father. Think about what is likely to go through *you* as you listen. How long will it be before you find yourself wanting to comfort him or correct him (for example, tell him what he should be feeling) or tell him your own story? Or before you want to change the subject altogether? Even your wish to comfort him may be a way of dismissing him, of ending the conversation.

Those who work in helping professionally know how hard it is to maintain a listening attitude. They know it is a goal that one works toward—to be able to listen better and better with less and less need to intrude. The same is true of anyone who wants to listen: Make it a *goal* to maintain a listening attitude.

Rule 2. Saying back—telling people what you hear them saying—is where the whole process begins.

Eugene Gendlin has said that the basis of good listening technique is "saying back." This can be done either in a person's own words or in your own, but the goal is to catch the *crux* of what a person is saying and to say it back.

Simple as it sounds, the technique has some startling benefits. For one, it requires the listener to pay attention to the speaker's thought and not his or her own. Second, it makes survivors feel heard and reassured that the listener knows what they are talking about. Third, and of course most important, it allows the person being listened to to carry his or her thinking—and feeling—forward to the next step.

Often, even by only literally saying back the words that have just been said to you, you give people the chance to hear themselves and the chance to extend and expand their own experience of the meaning of things.

(In addition, saying back is not hard to do. The hard part is remembering that that is where the helping process begins.)

Let's take an example.

A woman in her fifties is in pain. Her daughter has killed herself. Clearly upset and depressed, she says to you, "Why? That's what I can't understand: Why did she kill herself?"

You resist the temptation to answer the question itself or even to calm her down. Instead, you reflect the essence of what she is saying right now: "You're really puzzled by the why of this, aren't you?"

How does this help?

It picks up on, and encourages, a shift in emphasis from the pain the woman is experiencing to the puzzlement she is expressing. It opens the way for the next step, perhaps for the recognition that there is a puzzle, and it opens the way for a further exploration of the puzzle.

What is so puzzling? That her daughter was in such distress? That she had to kill herself? That there was no other solution that occurred to her? Or is it that the survivor wonders whether she herself failed to do something she should have done? The listener can't know, but he or she can help the person find out.

The survivor says, "Yes, it's just how desperate she was that I don't understand."

You say, "You don't understand her desperation."

She says, "Her desperation seemed so out of proportion . . ."

You say, "It is hard to understand what her thinking was, isn't it?"

Now the way has been opened up for a discussion of her daughter's thinking, perhaps the nature of her daughter's illness and so on. The focus has moved from the *survivor's* pain, through puzzlement, to a discussion that can now focus on understanding and clarifying the

149

daughter's frame of mind. Things have changed—although, clearly, the discussion, and the pain, aren't over.

Rule 3. If you get stuck or if you don't get it—say so.

Try to say which part of the speaker's thoughts you *do* get and which part you *don't* get. This has a way of encouraging the speaker to clarify what he or she is saying (which, of course, is the whole point).

The woman goes on. "She seemed so desperate to tell me something. All those things she said to me didn't add up. I just keep wondering."

You say, "I get what you're saying about her desperation. I don't get it about all the things she said to you and your wondering."

She says, "Was she sending me a message—about me?"

Now the way is open to talk about what went on *between* them. Asking the survivor to clarify has helped her focus more clearly on what she needs to talk about next: their relationship.

Don't hesitate to ask someone to clarify if you don't understand what he or she is saying. Pretending you understand is of no help; they'll catch you soon enough. And asking them to clarify helps them.

Rule 4. Another way of giving something is to say what you *are feeling as you listen.*

You can say what you are feeling about the speaker or what you are feeling about yourself. Try to put it positively, but be honest. Your aim now is to give a *reaction,* not advice, not words of comfort; to provide the sense that the survivor has been heard and is being responded to. The point is not to intrude out of your own need to express yourself, but to give something that will help someone else carry his or her own thinking forward.

For instance:

"When you talk about your daughter like that, I feel sad and puzzled, too."

Or:

"You make me think of my child and how I'd be out of my mind if he did that."

Or (and this begins to move to still another kind of response, Rule 5):

"When I hear you talk like that, you make me wish I could help you better."

Rule 5. Sometimes it is possible to talk about what is going on between you and the survivor.

This is a particularly intense form of sharing your response. It makes a person immensely aware of his or her own communications. It can be very valuable, but it has to be handled with tact as well as honesty.

You could say:

"You know, you always come to me with your sad feelings. It makes me feel good that you think I can help you—but it makes me sad, too."

Or:

". . . but it makes me feel guilty that I still have my son and you don't have your daughter."

Or, even:

". . . but I think you expect too much from me. Maybe you need more help than I know how to give."

It is important to remember about this kind of responding that it is still a way of listening. You are listening to the effect that somebody is having on you. You are sharing your experience, your feelings, or your sense of the interaction between you *as a way of helping someone else to focus, clarify, and understand his or her own experience.* The listening attitude is all-important here.

Rule 6. Look for shifts in meaning.

It is important to remember that as a listening helper you are not necessarily looking for agreement that what you have said back is correct. You are not even looking directly for verbal expression that somebody feels better. You are not looking for thanks (nice as that feels). You are looking for evidence that there has been some shift in meaning. Things seem different, if only temporarily, for the person in need. That is the sign that something really helpful has taken place.

One of the reasons why serious help is difficult to offer on an ongoing basis—and why a professional is often needed to pick up the task—is that all the ordinary signals and rewards, such as "you're right" and "thanks for making me feel better," have to be willingly given up by the serious listener. Nice as it is to hear these, and appropriate as it is to expect to hear them *eventually,* you cannot rely on such feedback. The only real sign that you have been helpful is evidence that the other person's experience has moved forward.

Rule 7. Be prepared for things to move slowly.

The rules described above obviously simplify a complex process.

151

Remember, your job is to facilitate a difficult, complicated, and often painful working-through. The same ground may have to be covered all over again. And then all over again! Meanings change slowly. Be patient.

Rule 8. Be prepared to back off.

Sometimes, when you get the signal, you will just have to back off and wait. Often people need time and space to work out privately a process that has been started by talking. If you get the message that this is what is needed, then let the person know that you are there, that you respect the need for space, but that you are ready to listen again when he or she wants to talk.

SOME ADVICE ABOUT LISTENING

Practice listening. You will be surprised at how little listening we all do as part of everyday life. It is a forgotten skill, one that we neglect in our eagerness to think about our own experience. Often we talk because we want to find out what our own lives are all about. Helping is different. We are reminded of a psychotherapist whose twenty-year-old patient killed herself. The psychologist felt guilty and said so to his colleagues. They hastened to reassure him, to remind him that he was only one influence in her life, that she had a will of her own, that no one controls another person's life, and so on. As he listened to the warm outpouring of his concerned friends, the psychologist got more and more depressed and more and more angry. "If only they had let me talk about how *I* feel," he said, "instead of cutting off my guilt." In fact, ironically, his colleagues were doing with him what they would never do with a patient.

Take the opportunity to practice listening in everyday situations. Follow the rules we've given. You will be a much better helper when you are called upon. And you will find that your everyday exchanges are deeper and more connected.

TO SURVIVORS

When you want help, find a listener. Some people are better at it than others. For whatever reason, they are more willing to put aside their own needs to express themselves. They know enough not to offer empty advice. They know how to offer you their company in such a way that you make better sense of things when you are with them. Find somebody who you feel *hears* you and understands you. Talk to him or her.

You can even let people know, quite directly, that you only want them to listen and to tell you if they understand, to say what they hear you saying. Tell them you are not asking for advice, solutions, or even comforting words. Tell them that you just want them to listen.

If you can't find a good listener (most friends are good up to a point, and then their own needs take over), you may need a professional one. You may need someone who is trained to help you make sense of things and who knows how to keep from imposing his or her own thoughts, feelings, and values on you. But, in finding professional help, be guided by the same criterion: You want somebody who hears and understands you. If not, whatever their training, their help may be irrelevant.

Some Advice About Advice

As a survivor—and someone in distress—you may be tempted to think that what you need goes beyond simply being listened to. You may think you need something more active—someone to take your problems on for you, someone to tell you what to do.

Of course, advice has its place. Legal or financial or medical advice, for example, may be important psychologically (as well as legally, financially, or medically). Advice may make you feel taken care of and make you feel less alone. In times of stress we do need to feel taken care of and less alone.

But, be careful. Advice, if it is to be any good, depends on the advisor's willingness and ability to listen to *you*. Make sure your advisors are listeners. If they aren't, their advice is more likely to be about *them* (that is, what they would want if they were in your place) than it is to be about you.

153

Chapter 15

GETTING HELP BY TALKING

I cannot express to you how wonderful it was to be able to talk to her; part of that endless, incessant outpouring of feelings that I now know is necessary.

—A SURVIVOR

What cannot be cured or changed can sometimes be borne more easily. Bearing tragedy more easily, we have said, involves being able to respond with one's own natural, self-corrective mourning process. This is what being helped is all about—finding a climate in which the self-corrective process (the process by which you feel just a little better about things, a little less depressed, a little less stuck) moves forward.

And the crucial thing about such a climate is having the opportunity to be heard. To talk and to be heard.

Many survivors arrange to be heard by agreeing to listen to each other in self-help groups. Others arrange to be heard in psychotherapy. Some families agree to get help hearing each other in family therapy. This chapter is about these kinds of help.

THE SELF-HELP GROUP

Over the last few years, in many places across the country, suicide survivors have gotten together, often with mental health professionals such as social workers and psychologists, often without, to form discussion groups in which they can air their woes. The concept of such groups is not new. Alcoholics Anonymous is perhaps the oldest and most famous, but there are many more. At the New Jersey Self-Help Clearing House, for instance, we saw a computerized list of hundreds of such groups, in all areas of human suffering, from battered wives to diabetes to suicide.

For the most part, survivor self-help groups function alike: Many, for instance, start out the evening with a simple potluck supper to which everyone brings something. Talk is general, as people catch each other up on where they have been during the previous month. New members are introduced at this time.

Then, at a typical working session, which lasts for about two hours, members take turns telling about themselves. Going around the room in order, each person will introduce himself or herself, tell who it was who died, when it happened, how it happened, how he or she is feeling. For a while there is no response, with each survivor listening respectfully to the other's story. Then, as someone stops, perhaps caught up in tears or grief, another member or the group leader may say something. It can be as simple as "Yeah, that's the way I felt." Or "Let me tell you what happened to me."

Guilts are shared. Some rush to excuse each other, though often someone will say, "If she wants to feel guilty, let her. We all do."

As the evening progresses and the circle has been closed by the last survivor's story, the discussion becomes looser. Someone may remember something he or she didn't say. A comment is made. A question is answered or asked. "Why?" is a frequent question. "Why didn't they tell me?" "Why didn't the doctors do something?" "Why won't my grandson talk about the suicide?"

Some groups are for all kinds of survivors; others have a more specific focus. Most groups accept anyone who wants to get in, though some have interviews ahead of time to inform people of what it is they can expect from the group.

MARTHA:

In my community, there are two different groups. One is for younger suicides and the other one is for older suicides. The one we'd gone to for a while was the younger. The people at the group are very positive. They're all various points past suicide. Some a month, six months, two years, fifteen years. It's led by two women, and they both have suicides in their family—their brothers committed suicide—so they really can understand, besides being psychologists and understanding from that point of view. This month we went to the group for older suicides. They are people who have also lost a mother, a fiancée, a father. It's nice just talking to people who understand.

The deep importance of talking to people who understand your feelings is echoed by almost all survivors who have had the experience of going to groups.

SARAH:

I felt it was good, because here are other people who have gone through it. I didn't want to talk that much at home because if Patricia felt good that day, I certainly didn't want to burden her, and she usually felt the same way, and my father too. So I'd rather talk to someone outside. I felt I wasn't burdening the people in the group. They were very supportive.

But there are other reasons why groups seem to help people.

"Groups allow us to share our grief."

"We can overcome stigma and shame there."

"It's a safe environment in which to share pain."

"It reinforces our self-esteem."

"It gives us support models."

"It tells me that grief is okay."

"Mutual support helps us to deal with the myth that 'If only

157

I'd done something different, made him feel more loved—he'd have lived.' "

"It helps to cry and not have people stop everything they're doing."

"People need to know they're not crazy. The group gets rid of our fears about behavior and fears about having fears."

Some self-help groups are led by professionals with mental health training, or a background in counseling or in group work; others are led by lay people, survivors themselves, eager to help other survivors.

While there is some argument about which kind of leadership is better, everyone agrees that the personal qualities of the leader are critical in making a self-help group experience effective and valuable. Some feel that professional background and training is a must and that it takes expertise and sensitivity to maintain a climate in which real help can be obtained.

Some survivors, on the other hand, feel very strongly that just being a mental health professional doesn't qualify someone to lead a group of suicide survivors. They claim that groups have shown they can work very well without professionals, who often (they say) don't seem to understand the kind of grief survivors go through.

Whether professional or lay person (some groups have both), the necessary quality of the leader, like the quality to be looked for in any helper, is to be able to listen and to be able to help group members *listen to each other.* And this of course goes to the heart of the matter of the group's effectiveness. This is because, most important, groups are a way of being heard—of sharing experiences with people who will understand those experiences and who will be sympathetic.

Self-help groups are effective for other reasons, too. Self-help groups encourage an activity which facilitates the mourning process in one's self—the activity of helping others. "I heal as I help," one survivor told us.

In addition, a group is a place to remember the person who died, to talk freely about him without feeling the constraints society and friends impose. Most people also seem to agree that survivors can use groups to gain reassurance and support, to get rid of misinformation, and, by seeing that others are going on with their lives, to become "unstuck" themselves and to take inspiration from the fact that other survivors are going on with their lives.

Self-help groups do have limitations. Some survivors have severe problems that existed long before the suicide—problems that the group just can't heal. Some people have depressive disorders which need psychiatric attention.

Also, some people have a tendency to impose themselves and their needs on a group in a way which can become manipulative or dominating. In the absence of a leader who is skilled enough to handle such people, one person's own brand of "stuckness" can become a real problem—for himself and for the whole group.

So, if a group isn't working as well as a survivor wishes, it's worth looking around for another one—or for an alternative form of help.

We live in a world in which suicide survivors feel isolated and alone. Silent grief deepens that isolation. Anger and guilt make it worse. Isolation grows upon itself. Self-help groups are one way of breaking out of the isolation, and of allowing a healthy mourning to take place—with other people who have been through it too. Self-help groups can be effective and important. We only wish they were more available.

But, as of this writing, there are barely 150 self-help survivor groups in the whole country. Their average membership is 35. Their average monthly attendance is 18. That means that only about 4,500 survivors are being served, and only about 3,000 attend regularly—out of an estimated 600,000 new survivors a year. It seems that the bargain of silence is such that survivors don't even seek each other out.

MARTHA:

I just think that one thing that upset me was the lack of help available for survivors. I mean the fact that I have to drive an hour and fifteen minutes to New Jersey because there's no group in New York City, a metropolis of eight million!

I'm a pretty persevering person and I made calls—a conservative estimate is fifty calls—and ended up really getting nowhere until I was told about the group I'm now going to. That's just terrible, because I know that most people are not as persevering as I am. If they don't get it within one or two calls, that's going to be it. There's a lot of people out there who need help and who aren't getting it. Nobody realizes the devastating effect.

159

In the appendix to this book we list places across the country where survivors can find support groups.

PSYCHOTHERAPY

As valuable as self-help groups can be, it is often true that people—and people without severe problems—need a level of attention and sensitivity that a self-help group may not be able to provide. They may need the clarity of focus, the patience, and the tact that only a trained listener, a skilled psychotherapist, can provide.

Many survivors are reluctant to make use of psychotherapy, however. Indeed, while many go to see a medical doctor about some physical ailment in the first few months after the suicide, few go to see a psychotherapist. Many don't understand that they have a legitimate need for such help. Or that they are entitled to such help. Others don't *ask* for it—silent in grief, their silence extends even to asking for help.

Other survivors express anger (often quite bitterly) at mental health professionals.

Sometimes, as we said in chapter 6, the anger at doctors can be a kind of scapegoating. Sometimes, it is an outgrowth of bitter disappointment. After all, the mental health profession, to which they have turned for help in the past, seems to have failed them and to have failed them terribly. It did not keep their loved one alive.

In part, then, this angry reluctance to seek psychotherapy involves real disappointment. And it is a disappointment that professionals have some responsibility for—often they have allowed themselves to promise more than they could deliver. Often they have taken on the task of "treating" someone who is really not treatable, or they have not been clear enough or properly humble about the limits of their own capability.

But disappointment about the failures of the past can lead to an unfortunate misunderstanding. Survivors sometimes think that because the mental health profession could not save their son or daughter or mother or father, that it can do nothing for them as survivors. In this the survivor is wrong, because the situation is really quite different.

160

One: Most of the time, the psychological problem of the survivor is very different from the psychological problem of the person who committed suicide. Two: The kind of treatment required—talking psychotherapy—is different.

As for psychotherapy, it is worth remembering that the talking that goes on in the therapist's office is more like a kind of education than a kind of medical cure. It is an educational process aimed at clarifying experiences, correcting misconceptions, relieving anxieties. A psychotherapist promotes emotional growth the way a teacher promotes intellectual growth, for example, by asking good questions, by helping the patient to work out his or her own answers, by listening to the patient, by pointing out important connections the patient may have missed, by making the patient aware of his own tendency to get in the way of, or to ignore, his own good answers.

This kind of activity, like a good education, can be enormously useful in helping people to transform their own lives. But it can be terribly inadequate when it comes to solving other kinds of problems. If, for example, someone has a chemically based depression, no talking cure will help enough.

But a survivor's grief is different from a suicide's depression—at least most of the time. Survivors are not, by and large, "sick," that is, they are not psychiatrically ill people. They are healthy people going through an extremely difficult process, suffering an adjustment reaction to a severe stress—the Posttraumatic Stress Disorder we talked about in chapter 2.

Survivors are not necessarily suffering from deep neurotic or psychotic problems arising out of early childhood disturbance, or experiencing the symptoms of a biochemical disease—problems where the effectiveness of psychotherapy, as we have said, is often quite limited. In fact, rather, they suffer from the kind of problem that psychotherapy is most effective for—an adjustment reaction arising out of a specific and recent event. What's more, the sooner after such an event people seek help, the more effective that help is likely to be; the longer they wait (and the less they talk), the harder it is to help them.

So there are some things survivors ought to remember about psychotherapy:

Getting help depends on getting a good listener. Psychotherapists are trained listeners.

Think of psychotherapy as a kind of education (not as a medical cure). You learn to see yourself and the things that have happened to you more clearly—and more comfortably.

As in education, better, brighter students do better. Perhaps it's sad, perhaps it's ironic, but it's true—healthy people get more from psychotherapy than sick ones do.

Survivors, mostly, are healthy people suffering from adjustment reactions. As such, they do well in psychotherapy.

The sooner you get help, the better. The longer you wait (and the less you talk), the harder it is for a psychotherapist to help you.

Psychotherapists are trained listeners, but they are also people. You are bound to like and feel better with some people than with others. Find a therapist you feel good about. Above all, find one who really seems to understand what *you* are talking about.

FAMILY THERAPY

Sometimes families, even loving families, find themselves at an impasse—family members unable to help each other—stuck in an angry deadlock or frozen in their inability to deal with grief.

In family therapy, the whole family goes together to the therapist, who helps them to talk to each other. As they talk together, the therapist helps them to clarify their communication and to understand their interactions with each other. Problem patterns of behavior (like hidden alliances, or misguided loyalties, or overprotective reactions, or a wide variety of other unwittingly unhelpful exchanges) can be pointed out and corrected.

Family therapy is usually thought of as a short-term method—six or eight or a dozen sessions. It can be of great help in unsticking a stuck family. It can be particularly helpful in altering or undoing the bad bargain in a survivor-family.

MOVING ON

But how does a survivor know when to seek a psychotherapist's help? When, in other words, is a self-help group not enough? When are the untrained but sympathetic listeners at home not enough?

Do you feel better? Is the grief less bitter? Have you begun to give up the idea that you're the guilty party? Are you less angry? Can you, as one survivor put it, feel that . . .

> It happened. I'm sorry it did. I wouldn't have chosen suicide for them or myself. But now it's over. I've washed my hands of it. I'm free. It's time to get on with my life.

On the other hand, is there a litany that can't be broken? Have five years gone by and you still feel bitter, sick, depressed? Are you still having trouble getting back to work? Are you still making suicide the center of your life?

Your answer to these questions will help determine whether some other form of help is indicated. Trained listening can open up a process that facilitates recovery and is very valuable for lessening the pain suffered by suicide survivors.

HOW TO FIND A THERAPIST

Finding a good therapist sometimes takes a little doing. The best source is a recommendation from someone you know and trust. People who have been in therapy themselves are a good source of recommendation. If they have good things to say about someone they have been in treatment with, and they know you and think you and that

163

therapist would get on well together, that is a particularly good place to start.

There are local professional organizations of social workers, psychologists, psychiatrists, and nurses which you can call. They'll be happy to make recommendations. So, too, will local universities with social work schools, psychology departments, medical schools, and so forth.

You should also know that there is nothing wrong with making appointments for a first interview with several potential therapists—and picking the one you like best.

"OTHER THERAPISTS"

It's easy to fall into the trap of feeling that *no one* will listen. Sometimes it's just a matter of trying harder to find someone. For instance, in our conversations we have heard how some survivors were greatly supported in their recovery process by people both inside and outside the family. These survivors were neither in support groups nor with psychotherapists. We call their supporters "other therapists." They are people who can be there for the survivor when others aren't, in much the same way that, in normal life, one family member or another often is willing to listen and understand when another is not providing what we need. After all, no one person can ever give us what we need at every moment, but *some* family member or friend can listen to us, can allow us to express our anger or sob our grief, can be an "other therapist."

The National Academy of Sciences, in a study reported in *The New York Times,* said that a confidant is particularly helpful during mourning. When a survivor is alone, he or she carries on a conversation with the dead person, whereas with a companion, the survivor is more likely to talk over the meaning of the loss and about how his or her life will now have to change. Such confidants are "other therapists," as was Wanda's friend (in chapter 14) who "just listened." The best "other therapists" may be your extended family doing the kind of thing that Sarah and Dave tell us their families did.

DAVE:

I think having as many kids as there was made a big difference. There was always another shoulder to cry on, just someone else to help draw your thoughts away from the incident. A lot of the needs in companionship, the love that you want from one person or another—it helped that there were that many more people to take up the slack.

SARAH:

My boyfriend took the whole week off. He was there for me. In fact, we were all supportive, trying to tell each other that "it wasn't your fault, don't feel guilty. Don't feel blame at all."

We were close to begin with. There was already a relationship. And we said, you know, it happened, and it's nobody else's fault.

As can be seen, survivors themselves can be "other therapists": a father or mother helping the others through the difficulties of losing a child; a coleader of a self-help group; a sister or a brother of a suicide. One thing such "other therapists" have noticed is that helping others brings a large share of relief to their own pain.

A SOCIAL WORKER/SURVIVOR:

There was this couple in Colorado who lost a son. They've been going around telling everyone about how to know when your child is suicidal, alerting people to the danger signs. He— the father—told me how good it makes him feel to be active, to be *doing something.*

A MOTHER:

On Tuesdays and Thursdays I go down to the house of this older couple whose son killed himself. He'd lived with them for years. Maybe it's the "parenting" part of me, or maybe I feel good because I can take care of somebody—and make it work this time. Whatever, helping them helps me. Of course, it could be I'm just trying to make up for past "wrongs," but I don't think so.

165

A SURVIVOR WHO STARTED A SELF-HELP GROUP:
It's a way of making a meaningless death meaningful.

We can only wish that for every survivor there will be not only someone who is there for them, but someone for whom they can be the "other therapist."

Chapter 16

TALKING WITH CHILDREN

Adding to a child's shock and confusion at the death of a brother, sister, or parent, is the unavailability of other family members who may be so shaken by grief that they are not able to discuss the death with the child. The surviving relatives should spend as much time as possible with the child, making it clear that the child has permission to show his or her feelings openly or freely.
> —The American Academy of Child Psychiatry

It is common for children to feel responsible for the suicide or think that they should have somehow prevented it; living with this burden may make them become depressed, passive, and self-destructive.
> —The Harvard Medical School Mental Health Letter

I have not seen, heard or read about any person who has lost a parent by suicide who has not suffered serious and prolonged effects.
> —T. L. DORPAT, a psychiatrist

There is a prevailing and unfortunate notion when it comes to talking about death (and especially when it comes to talking about suicide), that it's better to leave children alone to heal by themselves or that not talking to them at all is better than saying "the wrong thing." Or even that telling the truth about death can be harmful to young children.

With suicide, nothing could be more wrong. Indeed, leaving children alone is dangerous. And waiting is unhelpful. Later, problems are more difficult to undo.

WHY WE HAVE TO TALK WITH CHILDREN ABOUT SUICIDE

Children whose parents kill themselves often end up in psychological trouble, so there is a good deal of research on what happens to them. It might be helpful to summarize the kind of things that children go through after such a death. Most of what we have to say is about the young child, but it is applicable to young people into and past their teens. Here are some of the things that happen.

Guilt

Children are often said to have a "magical" or "omnipotent" view of things. They believe that their wishes change the world around them. Since all children (and many adults, too) are often ambivalent about their parents ("I hate you today, Mommy"), this omnipotent sense can be very frightening when someone dies. The child may think, "I was angry at Mommy, so she died," and it is very difficult to correct this incorrect fantasy; the younger the child, the more difficult. So it is not surprising that children whose parents kill themselves often end up not only upset and disturbed about their loss, but full of guilt. So guilty, often, that a child may refuse to talk about his feelings lest someone find out the terrible thing he has done (that is, *thought*).

Psychologists who work with children (or with adults whose parents killed themselves when the person was young) find that they have difficulty in persuading them that there is no way in which they were responsible for the death. They *feel* that they are to blame. In fact, children often feel they are responsible for the difficulties that led up to the suicide, too. And why shouldn't they? Many parents, especially unhappy ones, all too often unload the blame on the child. Even without a suicide note, such parents leave behind the notion that it is the child's fault that they killed themselves.

Ironically, guilt can also be a child's defense against the terrible feeling of helplessness that suicide brings on. If *that* could happen, the child seems to reason, then all sorts of other awful things can happen to me! Better that I accept responsibility for this terrible event; that

168

way I'm no longer helpless. In short, some children would rather feel powerful (and guilty) than helpless (and innocent).

Anger

At the same time, children—like adults—experience the rage of anyone who is suddenly abandoned through a deliberate act. Strangely enough, even if children don't know (because the family doesn't admit) that the act was deliberate, they *feel* it, and they are properly enraged.

But children often don't and can't feel comfortable with their anger. Sometimes, in one of the twists of thinking that is so typical of childhood, they think that their anger *after* their parent's death was responsible for causing the suicide. At any rate, the rage is often transformed into guilt or depression, or doesn't show up at all. A relieved parent who says "It's amazing, he doesn't seem to be grieving at all" should be more worried than one whose child is having tantrums. Silence here, as everywhere, is a danger sign.

Depression

Instead of feeling guilty or angry, the child may be depressed. The depression may interfere with the kind of mourning that needs to be carried on. It may get in the way of all normal feelings—and activities.

Denial

As we said, an absence of grief is not a good sign when a parent dies. It may signal that the child is hiding his feelings. He actually may not cry, may go on with life as if nothing had happened. All sorts of fantasies may be going around in his head: "My father ran away," "My father is on a trip, but he'll be back," "My mother will come back if I'm good." Anything but accepting the terrible truth: that the parent has gone away permanently. Such unacknowledged feelings may seem to disappear, but they do not really go away. They get buried, but they do not get relieved.

169

Long-Term Effects

As with adults, there are long-term effects of parental suicide, and because the child is not fully developed and is especially vulnerable, these can be quite serious.

Children may grow up with the belief that they are permanently unlovable. All children, in the early years, have some fantasies about one parent or another leaving them, often because of something they have or have not done or because they aren't "good enough." When suicide occurs, that fantasy becomes reality, and the child may feel himself permanently abandoned and permanently unworthy of being loved.

Some children grow up with a permanent fear of their own power to cause harm to those they love. Some grow up with a lifelong sense of guilt, and may go through life trying to hurt themselves as a way of paying for their wrongdoing.

SILENCE

MARTIN:

When I was ten, my mother killed herself in our house. The rest of my family simply didn't talk about it to us. They fought between themselves—bitterly—with all sorts of accusations. Looking back, I think my sister and I sensed what was going on and interrupted the others every time they tried to say something important to each other.

We were all so busy with denying things and with our anger that we almost didn't act like a family at all. We didn't hug or kiss or communicate about our real feelings at all. It was a never-never land. Almost impossible to believe. My sister developed stomach problems; I was afraid to leave the house— for years.

Compounding all the child's problems is the family's silence. With young children silence is especially harmful, because it not only de-

170

nies the child the healing aspects of the normal mourning process but obscures the real story of the suicide.

So, the Grand Bargain is extended to include the youngest survivors. But children are—sadly, ironically—the ones *most* in need of contact. They are the ones who really need to be heard, reassured, and talked with. They are the ones most vulnerable to, and most harmed by, silence. They are the ones who most desperately need to experience a proper mourning period.

Selma Fraiberg, a psychoanalyst who has written about her work with children, talks in her book, *The Magic Years,* about the effect of not allowing children to experience pain or to express painful feelings.

> In our efforts to protect children from painful emotions we may deprive them of their own best means of mastering painful experiences. Mourning . . . is a necessary measure for overcoming the effects of loss. A child who is not allowed feelings of grief . . . is obliged to fall back on more primitive measures of defense, to deny the pain of loss, and to feel *nothing.*

WHAT CAN BE DONE?

Despite the grim picture we've drawn, many children can recover from a parent's suicide. The key is allowing them to:

- Grieve openly
- Express their feelings about the dead person
- Discuss their feelings about themselves

The family's natural tendency to be silent must be overcome.

TALKING WITH CHILDREN ABOUT SUICIDE

Talking helpfully and truthfully with children about suicide is based on the idea that truthful information about suicide is crucial; and that children need help with clarifying their emotional responses to the truth—as they understand it.

Truthful Information

It's important to talk truthfully to children right from the start. If they don't have truth, they can never make sense of things—especially so important a thing as the death of someone they love.

If we hide things from them, there are always complications. Children tend to make up their own version of the facts and get lost in their own private, and potentially harmful, interpretation of reality. Alternatively, the child catches on, one way or another, to what has really happened and learns, early on in life, that he cannot trust the adults who are closest to him to be straight with him.

Expressing Feelings

It's important to help children to express and clarify their feelings as they respond to the information you give them. Healthy mourning—the process of accepting and adjusting to loss and getting on with life—depends on the expression and clarification of those feelings. It is impossible for a child to do this kind of processing all by himself.

Helpful talking with children is like helpful talking with adults. The task is to provide a climate in which the child's self-corrective process can go forward. That process involves an ongoing rhythm: assimilating information that has been shared and working through the emotional response to the information.

Once again, the key is listening. Patient, understanding, reflective listening.

Listening comes *first* because, in order to tell anybody anything, you have to know to whom you are talking. Good listening always precedes helpful talking. You need to know what someone is experiencing and concerned about, what kinds of words and concepts

172

you can use, and you can't know any of that unless you listen first.

This is true for both children and adults. But helping children is also different from helping adults.

Listening to a child is different because children organize their thoughts and express themselves differently. Their capacity to do these things, depending, of course, on the age of the child, is limited, and relatively underdeveloped. And when things get very difficult for them—as in the death by suicide of a loved one—their own capacity to organize and express themselves may not be up to the task.

Listening to a child may mean filling in the gaps. It usually also means paying more attention to the nonverbal ways children have of expressing themselves (their play, the way they behave, the way they seem to feel, the way they make you feel when you are with them).

Listening to a child involves making some guesses (educated guesses) about what he or she is likely to be feeling and thinking—and then seeking, gently, to find out if your guess is right.

Talking to children is different, too. They need more help making sense of things. They need basic information. They are more likely to misunderstand. They do not have all the words and they may not understand your words. They cannot help you explain to them what you are trying to say, the way another adult can.

To talk with a child, you need to know some things about the way a child communicates and some things about the way a child organizes his or her thoughts and feelings.

Children's Communication

Children often communicate nonverbally. Instead of talking, they act. It helps to try to figure out what you would be feeling if you were acting that way.

Freddie, aged nine, for some months—ever since his father's disappearance (which was unexplained to him)—had been doing everything in a painfully slow and energyless way. His mother could not get him to school on time, could not get him to finish his meals or to do his homework. She became furious at what she thought was his "dawdling."

His aunt came to the rescue. She could see at once what his

173

mother did not want to see: Freddie was depressed and in mourning. The mourning went unrecognized because the death had never been acknowledged. The death had not been acknowledged because no one could bear to explain to the little boy that it had been a suicide.

Children use words inaccurately or with special senses. It always helps to find out what they mean by the words they use.

Claire, a six-year-old girl, some weeks after her mother's funeral, kept saying, "I *hate* my grandmother." Everyone was puzzled by this, and her grandmother was hurt.

When someone thought to ask her what she meant by *hate,* Claire said, "She's sleeping in my sister's room and we can't play, and she cooks supper—yuch!"

It became clear that Claire meant that she wished her mother was still home and running the household, and not her grandmother. When asked about this, Claire said, "Yeah, I want her to just visit." She liked it better when her mother was there and her grandmother just visited.

How unfortunate it would have been to take Claire's word *hate* literally. She just didn't want her grandmother taking her mother's place.

Children express their feelings in their play. If we pay attention to what game the child is playing and especially what feelings are involved and what themes are expressed, we can get a line on what the child is going through and trying to say.

After the death of his grandfather, Howie, aged seven, became a collector. He collected all sorts of things, but especially things ordinarily discarded—wrappers from candy bars, half-eaten apples, bits and pieces of paper. His parents found these things in his room, under his bed, in his pockets. He became alarmed, angry, anxious, when his mother tried to throw them away.

His parents were so concerned that they brought him to a psychotherapist. Gradually, in treatment, the meaning of his play

174

became clear. He had come to believe that his grandfather had died because his life "was of no use anymore," a phrase he had heard from adults. He missed his grandfather and wished him back; he was frightened of still more losses, especially of losing "used-up" things, so he tried desperately to hold on to all he could.

Children who cannot say what they are feeling can nonetheless learn to evoke the response they need from those around them. It helps to pay attention to what *you* feel when you are with the child.

Sometimes a particular child makes you feel something that is *complementary* to what he feels. For example, if you feel especially protective and supportive, he may well be feeling especially vulnerable and needy.

On the other hand, children sometimes evoke a response in you that is *parallel* to theirs. They make you feel just the way they do. Especially angry children. They can make an adult—even one who doesn't want to—feel angry in a minute. If a child makes you angry, the chances are that he or she is angry.

Children's Thinking

Children organize their thoughts and feelings differently from the way adults do. Some aspects of their thinking are especially worth paying attention to with respect to suicide.

- They think concretely and have a hard time with abstractions. The child's literalness can lead to some frightening misunderstandings, as when the child is told that "death is just like sleep." A frightened youngster may not want to go to sleep for fear of dying.
- They think emotionally. That is, when trying to understand complicated ideas, they often rely on the emotional tone of the teller. They may sense that death is sad, frightening, dismaying; or, alternatively, that it is a peaceful, natural end; or that it is a relief; or that it is the outcome of a hostile act. It all depends on the tone in which they are told about it.
- They have a hard time understanding cause-and-effect relationships (as any adult who has tried to find out who "started" a fight

175

among siblings, for example, quickly finds out). And, as we have said, when the relationship between events is fraught with strong feelings—like the question of what caused someone to kill himself—children may well think in a way that some call magical.

• They believe that if they are good, the world will be good, and if they are bad, the world will be bad. So that when things go wrong, they think it's their fault. Or, equally unsettling, their belief in the *reliability* of the world is shaken.

What to Say to Children About Suicide

First, children need information. They need truthful talk. They need to know, in terms that make sense for their age, that someone died. And, if they are old enough, they need to understand that the suicide did it to himself. They need to know all this in the simplest, clearest, plainest, most concrete of terms. Death is death; it's not "going with the angels." For instance:

> Your mother (father, grandparent, sister) wasn't feeling very good about herself. In fact, she was feeling so bad about herself that she decided she couldn't go on living. So she killed herself. I know that sounds terrible, and it is. We all feel awful about it.

Don't tell him too much all at once. Tell him a little. The essentials. Then wait and listen. Ask if he understands. Ask if he has any questions. Tell him that if he has a question—now or ever—he should ask it.

In terms of whatever additional information he requires, the child will lead you to what is needed next.

And he will have feelings; you will need to respond to them.

There is a rhythm to the giving of information and the child's processing of that information. Sometimes children indicate a need to be informed and sometimes they simply need to work through their understanding of the information and to have their feelings clarified. As with adults, don't be surprised if the entire process has to happen over and over again.

Telling Stories

Sometimes, with young children, after information has been shared, the dialogue needs to continue in terms that are a little less direct.

For such children, storytelling may be more comfortable for everyone as a way of expressing and clarifying emotional responses—in much the same fashion fairy tales offer a way for parents to expose children to the intrigues of violence and greed, loss and despair, heroic and villainous behavior.

There are several forms such a story might take. We've made an attempt at two of them. Parents are much more likely to understand their own children and formulate their own version than we are, but the following are the kinds of tales we have in mind.

Analogy

Once children have been told about what actually happened in their own family, in real and simple terms, it may be easier, both for them and for the adult, to deal with the complex emotional responses by analogy. Children often find it easier to listen to the story of someone else's experience rather than their own, and they will often be able to use that story for their own benefit.

> I knew a man who killed himself; his daughter was just about your age at the time. She was really angry about it. You know what she said? She said that she wanted to kill her father. She said that she didn't care if he was already dead; she wanted to kill him for killing himself. And then, do you know what she did? She suddenly started crying. She said she felt so ashamed for feeling angry at her father who was already dead.

Especially for the child, it may be easier to acknowledge, clarify, and express ugly feelings if they appear in someone else.

> Another thing my friend's child thought was that it might be *her* fault—the death. Her mother told her, "It's not anyone's fault. Don't worry. Angry feelings *can't* kill people. There's noth-

177

ing you could have done. There's nothing any of us could have done. He just didn't want to live anymore."

Made-up Stories

For years, whenever her young children were sick or upset, a mother we know used to tell stories about a bear to them. She had found that they were much more apt to listen—and heed—her advice and comfort if it was couched in these terms. Direct, frontal approaches to psychological difficulties were met with a stubborn, defensive response. On the other hand, the children loved to hear these bear stories and often took great comfort from the solutions the bear found to problems that they themselves encountered in life. In a similar fashion, then, a young child may be able to handle some of the emotions aroused by this disaster through the use of a made-up tale.

The wonderful children's story *Babar* is an example. In the beginning, Babar and his mother, while traveling through the jungle, encounter a hunter. Babar's mother is shot, and little Babar has to go off by himself. The parents who read such a story to their five- or six-year-old child will notice that while this is a painful episode, one that the child finds sad, it is also a comfort to learn that it is possible to go through these unpleasant experiences and come out the other side, whole, alive, and able to move on. Babar, after all, grows up, meets Celeste and the Old Woman, and becomes King of the Jungle.

Such stories can be about a bear, a rabbit, or any other kind of animal, perhaps a familiar one, perhaps Babar himself, or Peter Rabbit, or some other imaginary creature. The story can be elaborated upon from day to day: It is the bear that feels terrible anger. It is the rabbit that feels guilt. It is Babar's adventure into a world in which a loved one is suddenly, mysteriously, missing. It is a little cat who cannot talk about its feelings to its father.

Lulled by the familiar form of a bedtime story told by a familiar adult, the child can often recognize and respond to his or her own feelings.

Adults also need to be open to and alert to a child's own way of expressing himself. Eventually, children find a way of getting around to the subject. One such child, ten years old, kept bothering her father to get her a dog. Their cocker spaniel had been given away when they moved from the country to the city. The father didn't understand what the child could want with a dog in a city apartment. Then, one day, he realized that it was the child's way of bringing up the loss she felt when a beloved aunt had died, a discussion that had been too painful when the actual death occurred. Luckily, the father had kept the door open, and now the child was opening it further.

Don't be too concerned with making intellectual and final "sense" of things with the child. It is only important that the story or the conversation open the way for future conversations, for listening to the anger and guilt and fear. (One teenage survivor of a sibling's suicide said, "I want my parents to remain open and available. I may not be ready to talk now, but please tell them to keep after me, so that when I am ready, they'll be there for me to talk it over with.")

Remember, too, that talking is not the only way to communicate that you care. Keep the door open for tears. Or for simply holding each other, resonating with the knowledge that each—child and adult— needs the other to understand how much his world has been shaken.

Finally, it is also important to remember that because, ultimately, the child makes emotional—not intellectual—sense of things, *who* you are and *how* you feel when you talk to a child can go a long way toward communicating what a child needs to hear. You don't always need to have the "right" words. You simply need to be there, keeping the communication going.

A SPECIAL CASE: SURVIVORS OF AN ADOLESCENT SUICIDE

Recently, there has been a great deal of attention paid to the suicide of adolescents in this country. The fact is that adolescent suicides have probably never represented more than 15 percent of the total. The fact is, too, that the rise in the adolescent suicide rate came to a stop about five years ago, and may even be slightly diminishing. But it's also a fact that adolescent suicides are now the third most frequent cause of death among that age group, and *that* is very disturbing.

What has received relatively little attention, however, is the reaction of the adolescent's friends and acquaintances to suicide. This book, stressing, as it does, the effect of suicide upon *survivors,* would be remiss if it did not comment on the problem of what to do to help the survivor of an adolescent's suicide.

One of the differences between the suicide of an adolescent and that of others is that, typically, the adolescent has lived psychologically as much and as intensely in his peer group as in his family. That is, adolescent suicides leave behind *two* sets of intensely affected survivors: their families and their friends.

Their families need special attention because the death by suicide of a child is so painful. We've presented one such case at length in chapter 12.

Their friends need special attention as well. This need is particularly urgent because the possibility of romanticization and contagion—an imitation of the suicidal act—is so high. Also, since friends can often be reached as a group, intervention and "postvention" are also possible.

A recent article in a professional journal devoted to suicide has paid specific attention to this situation. The author points out that, not surprisingly, friends of young suicide victims often feel burdened and guilty following the death. Often, for instance, they had an inkling that the dead person was considering suicide; they may think they didn't "do enough" to prevent it. The article suggests that "if suicide is 'contagious,' then here is a prime place to stop it"—in the community where it is taking place. What is being suggested is a theme that Edwin Shneidman, founder of the American Association of Suicidology, himself discussed: *post*vention as *pre*vention. Get to the adolescent survivor and you may get to the next victim of suicide.

Among the article's suggestions there is one, in particular, we welcome: Encourage the expression of feelings among the members of the group—meeting together as a group. This could take the form of a memorial service, or school-wide or neighborhood meetings to talk about the dead person. The object would be to keep a dialogue going: To prevent the kind of silence and shame that so often settles over people after suicide; and to prevent the kind of idealization and romanticization of the suicidal act that other adolescents are prone to.

Further, the goal would be to make possible healthy mourning for the friends left behind.

At the beginning of this chapter we said it was dangerous to let children remain alone with their feelings after suicide. But it is also important for us to say that there is good evidence that children can recover from the aftermath of a suicide if they receive support. If those around them can't—or won't—communicate, the child suffers; if, on the other hand, children are allowed to express their emotions, to talk about what happened, to say what they need to say within the family, and if they are provided with professional help when things go awry, they can go on to lead healthy adult lives.

Chapter 17

LIVING WITH SUICIDE—SOME
STORIES ABOUT RESPONDING

For most of this book we've been quoting what survivors had to say and then commenting—saying what we think survivors ought to know. Below, we change that routine and simply let survivors speak for themselves. You may recognize certain themes from earlier chapters, or you may find new insights yourself as to how these particular people managed to deal (or not to deal) with suicide.

SEAN:

My mother once said to me, "If Frank jumped off a bridge, you'd follow him." When I was younger, she'd said I was too quiet, too much like my father; she was afraid I'd end up like him. But she always treated me as if I was part of my brother, and I resented her for that. I'd just ignore her, look at her, not say anything. (Don't get me wrong, my mother's a very nice person; she was under a lot of strain at that point. I love her.)

When we were growing up, people thought I was the fol-
lower, but in a lot of ways I was keeping Frank alive for a long

time. We were into some very heavy destructive drinking, and I was getting tired of that, too. I wanted to go my own way.

So it was through his death, in a way, that I became stronger. I really thought a lot after his suicide. Do I want to go the same way, or do I want to make something of myself? I guess, subconsciously, I made the decision that I wasn't going to kill myself like Frank did. Something clicked in me that I can't continue on in a suicidal, symbiotic relationship. I guess I was a survivor.

My family has certainly been a stabilizing thing in my life. Marrying my wife has opened up a whole new adventure, too. She's South American, and we spent the last Christmas down there. A very warm family. That's been a whole "other therapy" too.

*

RUTH:

First of all, that last Wednesday, when she was home, it was in a sense saying good-bye. We spent the whole day talking. For a long time I thought she was just being difficult, being clever. She always intellectualized, discussed her *right to die* as a philosophy. As if it weren't an illness, you know. She'd argue with me, challenge me to argue with her, to tell her why one should live. I just got so angry at her. That last Wednesday, it wasn't at all like that. She wasn't argumentative. I could see that she was a broken person who was trapped within herself. I felt sad and sorry and worried for her, worried terribly that she might kill herself. And I did say good-bye that day, because we were talking.

After the first attempt I saw a therapist. Every time I'd come to that session, I'd cry. Six months of crying. I was mourning her. The therapist said, "She's alive." I said, "But for me she sort of died with that first attempt, because the child who I knew, who I thought I knew, who I didn't realize had that in her, had died." The child who was not suicidal was replaced with a child I didn't know. I mourned the healthy child.

So, in that sense, by the time she'd died, I'd already said good-bye.

I have a tremendous devotion to truth. I think you can gain a lot from it, from admitting weakness. Because then you find out if there are other people out there experiencing similar difficul-

184

ties or weaknesses, and when you share with them, you're actually helping other people with their problems. In the obituary for the local paper, we said Beth took her own life. That was something I had very strong feelings about, and Beth had strong feelings about it, too.

EVAN:

I think sitting shiva is so important. That went on for a long time. I was away from school for two and a half weeks in this house. It was as if time stopped. And, in looking back, that period went very quickly. In some sense you can say you were under constant attack (there were people around all the time), and I had some feelings of incredible loneliness, but for the most part there were people around you all the time, and you talked, because that's what you were supposed to do.

RUTH:

And we talked about Beth.

EVAN:

And it helped.

RUTH:

There is no doubt it's healing to talk to those who are willing to listen. No matter how impossible it seems.

EVAN:

I guess I would tell survivors to find people who will listen and not to blame those who can't.

*

WANDA:

I don't know if it's my attitude toward life, but there are some times that I think the suicide has done some things for me that might not have happened otherwise. A friend of mine said, you know, with some people, this could have really made them bitter and hardened or whatever, and with me I think it's probably made me more open because it made me realize that I would have to give up a pseudo notion of perfection—you know, some-

185

how "I can fix it." When I was younger, I clung to this image of perfection and having it all together. It has shown me the limits of my powers, I think, in a good way.

For me the hardest thing is to really have the courage to mourn openly, to talk with people about it. Some people put a stopwatch on me. They wanted me to be happy right away, but I knew that wouldn't work. I had to go through the grief work over and over again.

I think a lot about the importance of being vulnerable, and I think I feel stronger because I insisted on remaining vulnerable in this thing. You know, "It's better to bend than to break." After all, whoever says that life is not supposed to be shitty sometimes. I think that's a very spoiled attitude, I really do, and when you think about it or you read about the torture of people, I mean it would almost be sinful for me to be bitter when I've been so lucky.

There's something about knowing that you have hit bottom, and that it's hard. I feel like I have never been through anything like this in my life; it was, to me, the most horribly unimaginable impact, leaving me impotent and enraged. But I've survived it.

*

MARJORIE:

Don't misread me. I hurt, I hurt enormously. But I'm not bitter. My son told me one day, "I cannot accept it as you do, at least not now." Look, we probably will never recover as such. But we can still experience joy, simultaneously; not one overtaking the other. We can learn how to live with it.

I will never forget Rachel. I talk about her all the time. She is a part of my life and always will be. I don't try to close the door and forget she was there. She was one of the best things that happened in our life. Last year we had flowers in the church close to her birthday, and I said it was in remembrance of the beautiful things she brought into our life.

I don't think God is cruel. He doesn't want bad things to happen. He's here to help us overcome our pain. This is why I found the strength in church, in front of a packed church, to get up and talk. I was speaking *through* her. During the ten days between her suicide and the memorial service, I would

186

wake up at night and hear her words, which I had been thinking. And I gathered all her thoughts and it made my speech, and my speech came directly from this girl's mouth. I knew that too many people had too many reasons to feel guilty if they wanted to find reasons. But I didn't think they should, and neither did she.

*

SARAH:

There was never any blame in the family. We were close to begin with. There was already a relationship between me and my sister. You know it happened and you know it couldn't be anybody else's fault.

FRANK (her father):

Don't you find that what most things individuals do, no matter what it might be, is what they want to do, no matter what? Think about it: jobs, marriage, so forth and so on. Why shouldn't suicide be included as one of them? Why should that be someone's fault? Of course, no matter what happens, somebody likes to point the finger.

PATRICIA:

My boyfriend took the whole week off. He was there for me. But I don't remember him ever bringing it up. I guess people are afraid to. I guess that's what it is. And again I didn't want to keep bringing it up either. I don't know. I felt uncomfortable.

SARAH:

Didn't you almost sometimes feel like you were a burden?

PATRICIA:

Yes. You keep saying it over and over, and they don't understand. And if they say they do, they really don't. But just being there helps. It seems to get easier, but then sometimes it doesn't. You know, at work, mothers and daughters come in shopping, which is something we used to enjoy doing. And sometimes I have to go in the back and cry or whatever you have to do. I guess that'll always be there: memories.

187

SARAH:

I don't feel the anger as much anymore. Not all the time, like I did, every day.

PATRICIA:

Sometimes I get mad and think, "What the hell did you do that for?" I still don't figure it out.

SARAH:

But it's not every day. It gets easier.

*

RUTH:

I said what wouldn't we give to have my daughter back, and here I have my niece back because her attempt failed. She came back from the dead. How do we communicate with her that we want her to live? It's a chance I don't want to miss.

*

DAVE:

My older sister had psychotherapy; I know she went on her own accord. She went because she felt like she was unhappy and she didn't know why. She was going for approximately eight months and felt she wasn't getting anywhere and accomplishing nothing. But afterward she did seem a bit happier.

For a period of time I was having problems in school. I was goofing off, going to virtually no classes. My father, in agreement with some of my teachers and the guidance counselor, felt I had some sort of psychological problem that kept me from getting my schoolwork done. So I went from one doctor to another— psychologists, psychiatrists, psychoanalysts—they all told him I was definitely able to achieve and had no idea why I didn't. Then one time two doctors told my father that I was extremely depressed and they said that was the main factor for my not accomplishing my schoolwork. I didn't feel depressed. I felt fine. But I went to the doctors for a while. Eventually, I stopped going.

*

MILDRED:

After Mack died, I joined a group. He was on the tail end of that group of suicides, and being that he was twenty-three, they considered him still an adolescent, so the Mental Health Association got his name and called me. They said we intend to start a group. I think it helped. It was the only place I could go where everyone seemed to understand what I was going through. We all needed it so much they continued it beyond the eight weeks they'd intended. What happens is you find that everybody has the same feelings: "If I could have . . . " And while I've gotten over that stage, I used to think the same way.

There was a woman in the group whose son had killed himself. Hung himself. And she found him. She just kept repeating how painful it was. She didn't seem able to move off her guilt at all. And we couldn't help her either. You knew she hadn't done anything, unless she could read his mind. Seeing how useless it was for her to hang onto those feelings, you can see them in yourself and get rid of them.

I don't think anyone can be the cause of someone else's death.

There was another woman who said the suicide had caused quite a rift between her and her husband. She could not shake it. She was functioning, but it was still there. One of her problems was they used to call her Super Mom. It was her whole self-image that was destroyed, as being a good mother. Like my image of being a good wife was destroyed.

There was one sad case in that group. She was nineteen, and her mother was an alcoholic. Her mother used to call her up at two or three in the morning to come pick her up when she'd been out drinking; and she'd pick her mother up and say, "I can't keep picking you up at three A.M.; I have to go to school in the morning." There were two daughters, and they were very protective of each other, but their mother left a note that was really saying to them, "If you had been better to me, I wouldn't have done this." Oh God! Can you imagine someone hanging a trip like that on their children?

*

FRANCIE:

My mother shot herself just before dawn—and before spring—when I was five. I am now in my forties.

Silence—that was, until therapy, the major by-product of my

189

mother's suicide. My father was an alcoholic. So my grandparents adopted me. My grandmother was terribly depressed and never received treatment. My grandfather, who received the brunt of her rage, went to work, shopped, cooked, cleaned, and provided my sister and me with the fragments of joy that he could muster—a sandbox, a ride to the wealthy neighborhoods, some conversation, and jokes. He grew a mustache on demand, wore bow ties. My grandmother would fitfully mend clothes and fitfully make plans, but only in her late eighties was she reconciled to the loss of her daughter.

Initially, I would wake up before dawn and dress for school, anxious to avoid being caught napping again while my world fell apart. Then—terrible social anxiety and isolation. I was black, so that was already an isolator, but I remember the house dark, the blinds drawn, each member of the family in their respective rooms. Silence; and each one so alone.

From time to time I saw psychiatrists. One had told my grandmother to tell me about the suicide when I asked. But my grandparents didn't understand my compulsive explorations through my mother's belongings as a kind of questioning, so I learned of my mother's death in a peculiar way. At twelve, I spent the summer in Pittsburgh with family friends. I was forbidden to socialize with a nearby family of the wrong social class—a warm, welcoming bunch.

I was left with the only daughter of the editor of the local black newspaper. She was very spoiled. When I resisted some demand of hers, she exploded by angrily telling me that she only played with me because my mother committed suicide. I think I collapsed.

In addition to my struggle to overcome silence I have had to struggle with a vulnerability to anxiety; I have had to struggle with a preoccupation with, and preparation for, cataclysm—sudden deaths. I am just now learning to enjoy and embrace *this* moment, and to bow to endings, to embrace them, too, when they come. My mother's death was like being hit by lightning.

I have had problems with depression and thoughts of suicide since I was twenty-one, but I think my experience as a survivor—being on the receiving end—stopped me. When I taught fifth grade, I felt that I would hurt those children who loved and trusted me and that I would be betraying the values I advocated. After my nieces were born, the thought of them suffering and being bewildered, if I killed myself, helped me. My best friend's need for me has also helped.

I now think of my life as a precious gift that I am trying to learn to appreciate. In my work (I am a social worker) my difficulties and anguish have been a gold mine that has been an important resource for others. It makes some of the past and current pain worthwhile because it is useful for others.

Letting go, giving up my feelings of fear; crying—endless crying—it all helped, I think.

*

AMANDA:

I did some work a couple of years ago for that lieutenant governor, with parents of teenage suicides. I said to myself, "What am I doing here? This is insane." But, in a way, I got to like the people I was working with, and somehow I managed to work there until he resigned. And I was getting to work so I could cope, listening to the stories and trying to write to people and talk to people, and trying to be helpful. Even though it was a terrible subject, I was busy, and I didn't always think of it as suicide. I know that sounds funny, but I was thinking how to get this one on TV, what to do with this one, what kind of literature.

You know, I think it *did* make me feel better.

*

BETSY:

I couldn't get rid of the depression. You know what I mean? It was with me all the time. I got the idea that I just wanted to lie down in my bed and do nothing. I was living alone at the time, and my best friend came over and spent time with me, just taking care of me, feeding me nutritious foods, answering the phone. We talked about my father's death—over and over. My friend knew that I needed to talk, that I needed to have good food, that I needed to be a child again. Eventually, because, I guess, I was willing to let go, I let go of the depression, too. I began to heal.

People need to take care of themselves when things like that happen, physically, know what I mean? And if you can't do it yourself, then you best get someone else to do it.

191

*

MARTHA:

My mother and I had a chance to talk after she swallowed poison. I knew the pain she was in over my father's death. She had very good friends, but none of that was enough. She didn't have my father. And in a while we talked about "why did you do it?"

I'm adjusting to it now. I'm still angry, I'm still hurt. I think I'm beginning to understand her pain more and maybe rationalize it to try and understand it a little bit more. But I'm angry at her for doing what she did. It's like an abandonment; children who are orphaned must be angry at their parents: They've left you alone. There's all sorts of decisions you make that you always kind of talk to parents about, and now they're not here anymore.

It's an anger that she couldn't adjust to my father's death. Everybody else in the world gets widowed and they adjust. She just wasn't capable. I feel abandoned.

I enjoy my work. It is a very nice, rewarding feeling, helping people. Today I saw a patient that I haven't seen in six months, because I switched hospitals, who I had taken care of while she was on the ward and who came back just for a visit, and she looked great and she was so excited to see me and show me how well she was doing, and it was exciting for me to see her and to see how she really was doing well and she was adjusting to her stroke and she'd done a really good job, and it was nice.

I can't fathom people not having good relationships with their family. I always thought I was weird when I was growing up because I loved my parents. When I grew up, that wasn't chic. Everybody hated their parents and I was, like, "Well, you obviously are weird, Martha, you say you love them." To me, loving, including my extended family, is normal. So to me you have to have people to talk to, but I know there's a lot of people in this world who have no one to talk to and that's very sad. Because you really do need to talk to people about it. That's one of the best things that I find in the groups.

What did surprise me is how well I handled it. That I found very surprising. I would have thought that the death of *either* of

192

my parents would have devastated me. The fact that it didn't is surprising. I'm still angry and I'm still hurt but I'm working on those. Then, too, I'm wondering where my breaking point is. That I've handled it so well, so easily, has made me more fearful as to where the breaking point is. How much can I take before I crack? Of course I had work to do and I had responsibility and I couldn't fall into a hole and stop my life; that's not an answer either.

I was always an optimistic person. I think my mother knew that I would cope. She always said that she never worried about me. She worried about my sister but never about me. I was going to be okay. I've always gotten what I wanted. Not the easy way, sometimes the hard way, but if I decided that I wanted to do something eventually I would be able to do it, and that's just within me.

*

MILDRED:

This psychologist said to me: You can't expect to feel the same. Your children were part of you, and now they're dead. My God, did I cry! I mean, I was overwhelmed when he said that. He knew just how I felt.

*

WANDA:

We had a wonderful rabbi at the funeral whom I really liked. I wish I had taped the eulogy. He was very up front about my father's suicide. At one point in the sermon he said, "Fred Sherman committed suicide" and I remember my oldest brother, sitting next to me, cried out. It was good; it was not sugar-coated. The rabbi said there were all these people who cared about my father, I mean hundreds of people who showed up for the funeral; but my father didn't care about himself.

That was part of the funeral. How you are able to receive love and how you see life.

*

MAY:

I guess I thought about it off and on a lot, but I never really talked about it to anyone. As a matter of fact my brothers and I really hadn't talked about it much, and the first time I really

193

opened up was during World War II, so I was over twenty-one. I was working late in an office in Philadelphia, with my commanding officer, and something came up, and he started questioning me, and I told him the whole thing. It was the first time; so that was from the age of eight until twenty-one. And after that, it was easier.

That's funny. Before that, I had never really talked about it.

My relationship with Ralph is the most important thing; then our children—what they're doing, watching them develop and what's happening; and books. I read all the time—I mean I *really* read. I immersed myself in literature and I was lucky to have enough intelligence to know good literature. I went to the library when they finally allowed me to read the adult books, and I was so overwhelmed that I started up the *A*'s and I was going to read the whole thing. The librarian was absolutely aghast and she talked to my mother and said, "I can't let her take this book," and my mother said, "Let her take any book she wants." That was it more than anything, I really think. It may sound superficial, but I really think just being able to read saved me. And I have a lot of friends.

I guess I was lucky. I just had the right kind of personality or temperament.

I went through an awful lot of stages. I became very religious. I went to many different churches. I really looked very hard to find a religion that pleased me. I think probably the Friends were the most meaningful for me, and it was not that I was going to them looking for some solace or meaning for his life and his death. It was more trying to find a way of life, I guess, and an ethical ethos by which to live.

I owe a lot to Ralph. I think we've had a very, very happy life.

LUKAS'S STORY—
A PERSONAL SUMMARY

In the rest of this book we have written about other people who have been left behind by the suicide of a loved one. Here I pick up the story I started in the Introduction, my story. I do so not to make much of myself or my "survivorship" but because I think it may be useful, just as it has been useful for me to talk to others. Surely my experience with suicide is not unique; surely other survivors can benefit from learning about it and how—over the years—I have dealt with such a death.

The story will follow the framework of the rest of the book: first, the chronology; then the bargain of silence, my emotional responses, other bargains; and, finally, how I learned to respond with more of myself.

CHRONOLOGY

My mother had gone to her psychiatrist on an emergency basis that summer. She had become suddenly depressed while working as a counselor at a camp in Maine run by friends. Years earlier she had been diagnosed as manic-depressive and was receiving classic manic-depressive treatment of the 1930s, which, before pills, meant electro-shock therapy and patience. In addition, at my grandmother's insistence, she had been seeing a psychoanalyst. Then, that summer, at the age of thirty-three, she was too depressed to go on.

There she is, at summer camp, helping girls get their hair done in the morning, wearing bloomers and middy blouses with black ties, saluting the flag at sunup, watching the campers run about in their activities. The depression came on swiftly, and she returned home to our spacious Revolutionary era house in White Plains, New York. My brother was off at camp in Vermont, and I was playing with friends, unaware of the gloom. My mother's psychiatrist was on holiday, like all psychiatrists during August, but his home was in Connecticut, and my grandmother volunteered to come up from New York City and drive my mother there every day.

There had long been a feud between my father and his mother-in-law. She was, make no mistake about it, a domineering personality, someone who decided what was good for you—whether you were child, grandchild, in-law, or friend—and then saw to it that you did that. My mother was no match for her. Nor, apparently, was my father, who thought that Mother should have more shock treatment, not psychotherapy. (It is, of course, impossible to guess who was right. Nothing seemed to do much good. My mother's moods swung up and down, without much chance of control.) At any rate, that summer, the car, driven by my grandmother, ferried my mother to and from Connecticut for her daily fifty minutes. At the end of one session, my grandmother went into the house and, in violation of any decent patient-doctor relationship, set out to carry on a conversation with the psychiatrist about Mother. Mother went out into the garden. (It is, of course, unfair to suggest that this was the precipitating factor. Surely my mother's illness was well in place. Nevertheless, I want to convey to you what kinds of things roiled around in my head as I pieced all this together ten, twenty, thirty, forty years later.)

I believe my mother had made suicide attempts in previous years. I have been told that my father had been informed by the psychiatrist who had administered the shock treatments that "eventually" she would succeed. My father had had to live with that foreknowledge for seven years. That twenty-second of August, the waiting came to an end. Behind the psychoanalyst's house my mother found shards of glass and, in the kind of violent episode that characterizes so many suicides, cut her wrists and neck. She died soon after admittance to the local hospital. I have read the police reports, stuck away in my father's files; they are graphic and distressing. It is difficult to understand how anyone could inflict that kind of physical trauma on herself, no matter how much psychic pain she was in. Reading those papers, twenty years after I had first been informed about her suicide, was a decided shock.

All right, then, there they were, my grandmother in shock at the psychiatrist's house; my father, called from his office in New York City; my uncle, sent for from Baltimore, where he was doing his residency as a physician. What about me? They decided to tell me nothing, to send me to a friend in a nearby town. It was not unusual. Bobby and I had occasionally slept over at each other's houses. The next day, telling me only that my mother was "ill," my father and my uncle picked me up at Bobby's and drove me up to my brother's camp. The scene stays in my memory forever. I knew that something was unusual, for no six-year-old is sent off to camp without being allowed to say good-bye to his mother, with clothes picked for him and brought to his friend's house, in the middle of the summer. But nothing was said. She was simply "ill." In fact, she was already dead.

So, unaware of her death, I went to camp, arriving late in the evening, exhausted from the strange, long drive. I cried myself to sleep, homesick, frightened, lonely. The next day my father and uncle came after breakfast to bid me good-bye. Again I cried. My brother was there, but we didn't talk about this strange set of events. Ten days later, we took a train home and, at the station, discovered only my father in the gray Chevrolet. This immediately set me on edge: Where was my mother, why wasn't she there to meet us? The answer was given in the car. "You remember, when you left, she was ill? Well, she died." And that was it. No definition of the illness, no explanation. Not for ten years.

SILENCE

In chapter 11, when we discussed the Grand Bargain, we said that it was an agreement among family members that solved other problems, one of them being the pressure of feelings that were just too painful. It is better, the family thinks, to avoid discussion of the death than to bare those feelings. When young children are present, that becomes especially true, though—as we have suggested—especially harmful as well. In my family, the "conspiracy" of silence was certainly operative. There were several reasons for it.

Piecing it together, now, there was surely the agony my father was going through. He could not stand his guilt and anger, depression and grief. He simply could *not* talk about the death. His survivorship would be hard. Within a year, he had contracted tuberculosis, a disease now well known to be susceptible to psychological pressures. He would go away for a year to a sanitorium in the West. Later, like many survivors of suicide, he would become an alcoholic. He never learned to express his feelings about my mother's death.

But there was also the peculiar fight between my grandmother and my father. She wanted us to be told. I suspect that immediately set my father against it. Perhaps, in more rational moments, he might have agreed, and we would have talked.

So, the bargain between family members not to talk about the suicide was in full force. I did not violate its terms for many years, I did not make many attempts to penetrate the silence. Why? Because I felt the pressure *not* to ask questions. No one volunteered anything, so the rule appeared to be that you weren't supposed to talk about that particular death. (Maybe, too, I suspected that I might ask and be told things I didn't want to know: my own culpability in the death.) That silence has been maintained remarkably well for forty years. With rare exceptions, no one in my family has brought up my mother's suicide, though it has obviously had reverberations for all of us. In fact, the dictum of silence is so strong that I encountered numerous depressions and anxieties during the writing of this book. Only with a lot of soul-searching did I realize that they were due to the fact that I was breaking the rule of silence that had been established over forty-five years ago.

What were the other results of this silence? First, it prevented us from asking normal questions about the death. Mother's dying was a mystery, and normal questions were parried by mysterious answers. Second, we were unable to express our feelings. There was no catharsis, no mourning, because there was no memorial service, no funeral, no *evidence* of death. For a six-year-old that must have seemed particularly strange, since I knew that tears were usually shed over dead people. "No crying here" was the established creed. When my father got sick that year and went away—necessitating our departure for boarding school at the ages of seven and nine—we were supposed to smile and keep him unaware how miserable we were. To have mentioned our mother's death would have been uncouth and ungenerous. For me, however, it meant that I swallowed my pain. Tears did not flow. The hidden facts and the feelings we all sheltered from each other poisoned our relationships for years.

For myself, the silence led me to create myths about *how* my mother had died, where she was. In fact, I didn't believe she was dead. Why should I? Absent, yes, but dead, no. After all, I had no proof that she had even been ill. There was no medicine, no doctor, no body. And no discussion. Only a mystery. Perhaps she had been spirited away; or had left, on purpose. This must indeed be a very strange and dirty secret. Like many children, I invented ways in which she might have left and might, therefore, return. The silence provided a rich period for guilt and anger, none of which I was permitted to express at the time.

REACTIONS

Throughout this book we have talked about the anger, guilt, helplessness, depression, and other reactions to suicide. The curious thing is that I experienced many of those reactions even though, for ten years,

I didn't know my mother had killed herself. This suggests two things: Either that I had overheard conversations about my mother's suicide—in other words, I *did* know, but couldn't discuss it. Or that silence itself, surrounding *any* death, leads to the same kind of feelings.

Helplessness

The first feeling was of helplessness. If this could happen to me when I went away for a few days, then I was in deep trouble. I was afraid to leave my father's or my grandmother's or my brother's side. I was afraid to venture out into the world. After all, terrible things happened out there: People you loved disappeared.

Anger

Someone I loved had mysteriously left me. In fact, because I didn't know the truth (due to the silence), I thought my mother had *chosen* to leave me and was still alive. I was furious. But I could not express that anger because all around me people were in a curious, muted grief. My father was getting sick, and in effect I was told not to be verbal about my own grief, not to be unhappy (it might make my father sicker). By refusing to talk about the event, people around me led me to believe there was something wrong with *my* wish to discuss it. This led to further anger, and lots of guilt. The anger erupted in my early adolescence. I had "unexplained" tantrums. Later I could see they were the result of the ending of the fantasy that my mother would return.

Guilt

Feelings of guilt, too, lasted a long time. It's worth repeating what we wrote about in earlier chapters: The magical thinking of a six-year-old can lead him to believe that his anger can *cause* the death or disappearance of a parent. All children experience that kind of anger. I know I did. (After all, my mother had been depressed off and on, unable to care for me properly. Of course I was angry!) Now that my mother had disappeared, it was probably due to something I had done or thought or felt. Then there was that curious childhood rhyme from A. A. Milne. Remember?

James James Morrison Morrison Weatherbee George Dupree
Took great Care of his Mother, Though he was only three.

If James could do it, and he was only three, then why hadn't *I* kept track of my mother? That was the kind of thinking I went through during the months following my return from camp.

Naturally, all of this was pieced together by me years later, but there is a moment in a play by Ugo Betti *(Corruption in the Palace of Justice)* that expresses keenly how I spent my childhood. A young man is walking down a hallway. Someone behind him yells, "Stop thief." He faints. Later, a judge says, "You weren't the thief, why did you faint?" The young man says, "Because I always feel guilty." Everything in my life was tinged with the belief that I somehow had been responsible for my mother's death. Whenever a police siren sounded, I experienced a pang of guilt.

Helplessness, anger, guilt—the classic trilogy of reactions to suicide. Deep in grief, unable to go through the healing process of a proper mourning period, I experienced tremendous anxiety over the next twenty years.

BARGAINS

There were several bargains. In my childhood I decided, whether consciously or not, to become a "perfect" child. I think I believed that if I tried to keep from ever doing anything "wrong," my mother might come back; I might reverse time. The ramifications of this quite unnatural behavior (after all, what child should be expected to be good all the time?) were that I became very fearful of doing anything adventuresome, anything that might be considered inappropriate by my elders. In short, I became a cautious, housebound child, doing what I was asked, never straying far from righteousness. Not only did this result in a circumscribed existence, it often caused my peers to look on me with derision. Interestingly—sadly—this behavior continued on into early adulthood, even after I learned the truth about my mother's death. During late adolescence and college I continued to try to please everyone, to be the man in the middle. I continued to play by childhood's rules: I never stayed out late at night, I drank no beer or liquor, I didn't even cut any classes. In sum, I was a "goody-goody" in early childhood, a prude later on. I had killed off the playful, experimental, occasionally rebellious youth we all should have a chance to be.

Of course, this bargain won me a few things. My grandmother thought I was wonderful (a nice, quiet, old-fashioned kid). I stuck close to her side. I studied hard and learned a lot in school. Because I was so unadventuresome, I seldom got into trouble or got hurt, and I spared myself a great deal of the physical harm that I had, in fact, set out to spare myself. But what a price I paid in fears, shibboleths, anger, and grief. For I still mourned my mother, and I was unable to discuss her death, unable to express my feelings.

And I continued to believe that my father was lying. Something strange had happened. But what? If she was really dead, then either he had killed her or I had. Did I really believe this? Yes. The six-year-old's mind was carried forward into the adolescent's. With one part of me I knew I was not responsible. With another part, I thought I was. Of course this doesn't make "sense," but that's what often happens when anger is turned inward. I became a very depressed person. After all, like other suicide survivors, I felt that if only I had been worthy, my mother wouldn't have left me. I was stuck not only in my grief but in my young childhood.

You can see why, in chapter 16, so much stress is laid on telling children the truth, right from the beginning, and allowing them to talk about it as much as they want.

This attempt to be the perfect child was allied very closely with another bargain: control. Immediately after I was told that my mother had died (but not how), I decided that the adults in my life had obviously let things get out of hand. From then on, *I* would take charge. If James James Morrison Morrison had been able to take care of his mother at the age of three, then surely I, at the age of six, should be able to bring her *back.* I set about trying to control not only my feelings, by refusing to acknowledge the kind of anger and despair that a normal six-year-old has the right to feel, but to control the world around me as well. I set out to do what I felt the adults in my life had failed to do: keep people alive and well *and* bring my mother back from wherever she had gone. Naturally, I failed.

Then, one warm summer day, ten years after the suicide, my father, sitting at a table in a train station, waiting with me for the train that would take me to a vacation with my grandmother, said, "You know, don't you, that your mother killed herself?" "No," I said, "why?" "She was very sick." "How?" I asked. "Mentally," he said. And that was all. His self-doubt and guilt and shame and anger prevented him from saying more. My older brother had also been kept in the dark. To my dismay, when I started to discuss mother's death with him, I found that it was I who was informing him of its nature for the first time. So the search for truth and understanding began all over again. Suicide! It had never occurred to me during those ten years of solitary agony over abandonment. Why would someone do that? How, ill? What kind of mental disease? "She was psychotic," my uncle told me, that same year, as he lay on a lawn chaise in his comfortable Pennsylvania home, where, I thought, he could speak with amazing dispassion of his sister's manic-depression. It was another twenty years before I discovered that he, too, was ill; that he took lithium, went to "the Institute" for treatments, spent every day fearful of his own self-destructive instincts.

I went away to college. My studies had paid off, so I did well. But there, too, I continued to have problems. My relationships with my peers, with both men and women, were all affected. I did what May did. Assuming I would be rejected by women, I rejected them first, or got them to reject me. And I didn't trust men either. My father had lied to me, so other men would betray me. My mother had died, so other women would leave me.

I had physical symptoms, too. By the time I was twenty, I had developed severe stomachaches, so debilitating that I often couldn't go outside my home. They were especially fierce when I had a date. Then my bargain shifted a little. I wouldn't try to be perfect anymore, but I wouldn't have too much success, either—a kind of punishment for the guilt I still carried around with me. A survivor's guilt does not die young.

I graduated, getting high honors (all that guilty studying had paid off), and went to graduate school on the West Coast. Then, tiring of all studies, I headed for Hollywood and entered the television industry. In the years to come I made money, but not too much; I bought a car, but it couldn't be in top-notch shape; I had friends, but no close ones. I continued to feel punished, but I wasn't aware that it was I who was doing the punishing.

And I continued to ask, "Why?" Why had this terrible thing happened to me?

Meanwhile, over the years, silence was still the rule. I never asked my father about the suicide, and no one in the family brought it up. I still didn't know the details of what had happened (my father's file cabinet was ten years away), and no one else thought it important to tell me. Mind you, I continued to enter willingly into the bargain of silence. Was I mimicking my father in that, or simply using the bargain to avoid the painful guilt? Or was it simply that it was a shameful death, not to be shown to others?

At the age of twenty-two I entered a prolonged psychoanalysis. After several years, my stomach condition improved. So—more slowly— did my relationships with people. And I allowed myself to see that I was, indeed, very angry at Mother for having abandoned me that August day. Still, I held on to a belief that she wouldn't have done it if I'd been a better little boy. I also maintained a fantasy that someday she (or someone like her) would return to comfort me.

Gradually, things changed. I married. I entered educational television as a producer and writer. There I stayed for most of my career, working my way up into executive positions, watching as the originally modest medium grew into a multinational giant. My bargain was now that I would "do good" by making television shows for the benefit of the community.

Thirty years after Mother's death, my grandmother died, of heart failure. At her bedside was some medicine that was to be taken only in specified doses. The bottle was empty. Had she, in despair (over her own role in my mother's death, over her own lifelong depression), finally taken matters into her own hands? Strangely, I did not question the correctness of her suicide, nor was I angry at her. Perhaps I felt that by the time a person is eighty, she has the right to do anything she wants. Besides, there is a difference between abandoning one's family when one is thirty-three and doing it when one is eighty. But I was not to be permitted a passive role in these matters. Nineteen

204

seventy-nine. My aunt, wracked with lung cancer, went into a nursing home. My uncle, depressed, checked into the Institute. This couple, my surrogate "family," with whom Thanksgivings and Christmases had been spent, were dear to me. My aunt's ability to cope with a deafness that had its onset in her early thirties had symbolized noble resignation to me. Her home was the model of hospitality. Her four children received—it seemed to me—precious ministerings from her. Now, in the midst of terminal cancer—at the age of sixty-four—my aunt decides not to let pain and time make choices for her. She helps herself to death with morphine. The family discusses it; there are those who feel she had no right to deprive them of her warmth, her skill with life, her "motherliness." Others understand. I speak at her memorial service, but, as in the rest of my life, there is no mention of her choice in the manner of her death. No breath of suicide. We all choose to continue the silence.

Scarcely a year later, my uncle, recently out of the Institute, apparently upbeat and looking forward to his relationship with a widow he has met, locks himself in his bathroom, and, at the age of seventy, cuts his throat: my mother's mode of death. I am, once again, asked to speak at the memorial service. Why me? What is this passion for calling me to do this job? Am I qualified by dint of my own mother's suicide, or is it just that I speak well? My anger at uncle, aunt, cousins, grandmother, father, mother—*all*—is contained in the cocoon of depression that now encompasses me. Death seems to have no other face for me. My father, a confirmed alcoholic, dead from a failed liver and other organs, had been warned that any more drinking would kill him. Can he be said to be anything other than a suicide, too? Would my children, also, inherit this genetic wind? Would there never be any peace? I decide to talk about suicide. Finally.

MY RESPONSE

In part, this book is a way of taking control—by writing about suicide and trying to make use of what has happened so that others may be spared a little of the pain.

I feel that I have done more than survive. After all, I have never seriously considered killing myself; despite depressions that seemed never-ending, despite self-inflicted bruises of the psyche, I have not been doomed by the multiple suicides of my family. I now believe that my children are healthy, that the curse of suicide is not a genetic one to be passed on inexorably in my family. I am a survivor, but not one frozen in grief.

How did this happen, this change of heart? How did I cope with all these suicides in my family? While the answers are not necessarily valid for other people, they may be worth relating.

Other Therapists

First of all, despite the fact that my mother's death set off a number of other unpleasant events, I was not completely abandoned. My mother and my father had seen a school, some years earlier, which my mother (perhaps in a gesture to the future, cognizant of her own self-destruction) had thought "right" for us. It was there we went, to Vermont, after her death and after my father went away. It was a small private school, with only thirty-five students, and while it did not specialize in handling children of suicides, it was a wonderful place for outcasts of all sorts. The couple who ran it had a desire to make humans grow up with a wide range of abilities, and they loved children. Years later, I began to realize that, although I had been sent away after death—a terrible thing to do to a child—at least I had been sent away into an environment that nurtured all the special qualities that children have within them. I was encouraged to live life to the fullest—there, and at the Upper School, to which I continued in the ninth grade. I owe a good piece of my psychological wholeness to the music, drama, and philosophy of living I received at the Putney School. My mother, in her madness, had not been blind.

Other contributions to my survival: My grandmother, destructive as she was, believed that I needed to be protected, and protect me and my older brother she did. We stayed with her on vacations, received "care" packages from her at school, and were enveloped in her own brand of loving kindness. That that kindness was laced with guilt and anger was not consciously known to me, though I certainly felt that she was depressed much of the time. My father barely spoke to her; when he returned from the sanitorium, cured of his tuberculosis, we lived

206

torn between him and her. And yet, I must give her some due for the nurturing. No one can replace a mother, but my grandmother made the effort. As did other members of my family—supportive all: my mother's brother and his wife (the aunt and uncle who later killed themselves), my brother, my other aunt. They were "other therapists."

So was my wife. They say that getting married doesn't solve problems that you bring to the marriage, but I think that cliché was false in my case. My wife has been a crucial factor in my ability to survive, giving me strength when I lacked it, prodding me out of my self-pity, acknowledging the usefulness of psychotherapy, *and* giving me someone to care about. In my childhood I felt helpless, unable to make any difference in the chaos that surrounded me. Marriage to a loving and lovable woman made a difference: I was able to help her when she needed it, and I had someone to take care of and to care about. So, too, did my two children give me people to care about and to care for. Intelligent, warm, beautiful and—above all—healthy, my daughters have always given me something to live for. If having children does not always prove helpful for others, for me it provided one means of coping, a response to the suicides in my life.

Work

Finding an outlet can be a tremendously satisfying diversion from self-hate, fear, helplessness, and anger. Not make-work, but useful, productive, creative work. So it was with me. Writing, directing, producing television and film gave me great satisfaction and helped make my life meaningful.

The End of Silence

Finally, it is important to stress that the end of silence helped tremendously. When, at the age of sixteen, my father broke the news to me about my mother's suicide, it began to free all of us from the taboo of talking about her death. I was able, theoretically at least, to ask questions. Not just why, but any and all questions I chose to. Of course, at first, I didn't ask. I was too frightened, too shocked. But as the years passed, and I moved into my thirties and forties, I felt freer and freer to do so. Sorting out letters, memoirs, recollections, facts and myths, asking questions, talking about suicide were *all* therapeutic in and of themselves.

Then there was psychotherapy. I sought professional care. We have written about the need to have good listeners in self-help groups, in the family, with "other therapists," and with mental health professionals. Mine were excellent.

An *end to silence,* a *good marriage, creative work,* wonderful, *healthy children, psychotherapy,* a good school environment, "other therapists," and a good deal of luck—these are what I credit for my ability to cope with that devastating, shattering experience. Of course, I would be dishonest if I implied that I am a "cured" survivor. I still wake in the middle of the night trying to figure out the why and wherefore of that event of forty-five years ago. I still have anxiety. I still have my self-destructive moments, my angers, my guilts. I still feel strange talking about my mother's suicide. (It's the old taboo against talking; it's the hidden anger at those who abandoned me.) But I have given up some myths, too. I do not blame any member of the family for her death, including my mother. That realization occurred only this year, when I did research into Bipolar Affective Disorder. It is a disease, I've decided; and just as I could not blame my mother if pneumonia or cancer had taken her, I no longer blame her for killing herself. I am not as angry as I was.

In short, I do not feel stuck anymore. I do not grieve as I used to. I am no longer crippled by my mother's suicide. Part of my ability to respond has been created by the research and writing of this book. If it has helped no one else, it has helped *me.*

Christopher Lukas

The Future

Fifteen years ago, Edwin Shneidman, founder of the American Association of Suicidology, called for postvention, "working with survivor/victims of a committed suicide to help them with their anguish, guilt, anger, shame and perplexity." He said that "a . . . community ought routinely to provide postventive mental health care for the survivor/victims of suicidal deaths. *Postvention is prevention for the next decade and for the next generation*" (our emphasis).

Even back then, Shneidman estimated that there were at least 100,000 survivor/victims yearly—if one didn't count the disguised suicides. Today there are a lot more. But there is still no committed, concerted effort to "postvene." The silence continues.

It is very clear what is needed: an encouragement to talk, therapy designed for the survivor, dissemination of information about self-help groups, an end to the stigma of suicide—particularly as it applies to the survivor—and an understanding that there is a class of people called survivors. Surely suicide survivorship is a public health problem. Surely it makes good sense in the broadest social terms to stop the chain of debilitating illnesses, depression, guilt, and grief. It's time to end the silence.

Christopher Lukas
Henry Seiden, Ph.D.

Appendix

WHERE TO FIND
SELF-HELP GROUPS

What follows is a list given to us by the New Jersey Self-Help Clearing House and the American Association of Suicidology. Like all such lists it needs a little explanation. Self-help groups exist in many cities and communities. Some are led by mental health professionals or are associated with hospitals; others are led only by survivors; some are co-led. Like all lists, it is incomplete. Some groups didn't get on it because they didn't know about it or didn't respond in time. Other groups may have shut down by now because of lack of interest or financial support. So—if you want to join a self-help group and there isn't one listed for your area, try the following:

1. See if a local mental health association (or hospital or clinic) knows of other suicide survivors who are looking for the same thing.
2. Look for a regional self-help clearing house. In addition to those we dealt with—the New York Self-Help Clearing House, the New Jersey Self-Help Clearing House, and the Westchester County Self-Help Clear-

ing House—there are SHCHs in almost every state and county. This is a recent development (during the last five years) and a very welcome one.

3. See if there is a suicide hot line in a health clinic or run by the county or in a church. They may also have self-help groups. For instance, we note that the Dayton (Ohio) Suicide Prevention Center runs a very active Survivors of Suicide group; we note that San Diego Health Services and the San Bernadino County Department of Public Health have suicide survivors follow-up services.

4. See if there is a branch of the Compassionate Friends around. This group (much like the Samaritans in England) works with people who need support after a variety of deaths. Some of the branches run self-help groups for suicide survivors.

5. Ask the psychology department of your local college or talk to people at a nursing school or medical school. Occasionally, in the course of their training, mental health professionals run prevention hot lines or survivor groups.

SURVIVORS OF SUICIDE—INDEPENDENT GROUPS
(Alphabetical by State)

Survivors of Suicide	Mobile, Alabama
Mailing Address:	Robert L. Godwin, Jr.
	260 Jackson Dr.
	Mobile, AL 36609
Affiliations:	American Association of Suicidology
	Mental Health Association of Mobile Co.
Survivors of Suicide	Tempe, Arizona
Mailing Address:	Doris Sterner, R.N.
	2040 E. Loma Vista
	Tempe, AZ 85282
Affiliations:	Maricopa Co. Suicide Prevention Center
	SPC, Dayton, Ohio

East Valley SOS: West Valley SOS; Northeast Valley SOS
Groups   Tempe, Glendale, Phoenix, Arizona
    Mailing Address: Suicide Prevention Center of Maricopa
                    Co.
                    Dottie Deerwester, M.Ed., Director
                    1345 E. Main, #107
                    Mesa, AZ 85203

    Contact/Phone: Dottie Deerwester (602) 969-2783

Friends for Survival   Sacramento, California
    Mailing Address: Marilyn Koening
                    5701 Lerner Way
                    Sacramento, CA 95823

Heartbeat   Colorado Springs, Pueblo, and Denver,
                    Colorado
    Mailing Address: LaRita Archibald
                    2015 Devon
                    Colorado Springs, CO 80909

    Contact/Phone: LaRita Archibald (303) 596-2575
                    Pueblo (303) 545-2477
                    Denver (303) 777-9234

    Affiliations: American Association of Suicidology
                    Health Association, Colo. Springs, CO
                    Grief Education Institute, Denver, CO
                    Suicide Prevention Center, Pueblo, CO

Suicide Bereavement   East Hartford, Connecticut
    Mailing Address: Center for Inner Growth and Wholeness
                    P.O. Box 9185
                    Wethersfield, CT 06109

    Contact/Phone: John Mecca

Survivors of Suicide Support Group

	Winter Park, Florida
Mailing Address:	We Care Inc.
	112 Pasadena Pl.
	Orlando, FL 32803
Contact/Phone:	Jan or Marge (305) 628-1227
Affiliation:	We Care Inc.

Survivors of Suicide
Mailing Address:

Aurora, Illinois
Stephanie Weber-Slepicka
512 Liberty Street
West Dundee, IL 60118

Survivors Support Group

Mailing Address:

South Bend, Indiana
Shar Joyce
Survivors Support Group
706 South Ironwood
South Bend, IN 46615

STRESS (Striving to Reach Every Survivor of Suicide)

	Merrillville, Indiana
Mailing Address:	Mental Health Association in Lake Co.
	2450 169th Street
	Hammond, IN 46323
Contact/Phone:	Christy Markovich (219) 845-2720
Affiliation:	Lake Co. Mental Health Association

Suicide Grief Support Group

	Cedar Falls, Iowa
Mailing Address:	Keith Stokes
	828 West 4th Street
	Waterloo, Iowa
Contact/Phone:	Keith Stokes (319) 233-5538 (home);
	(319) 234-1724

Seasons: Suicide Bereavement

	Bethesda, Baltimore, Maryland
Mailing Address:	Coryne Melton
	13907 Vista Drive
	Rockville, MD 20853

Douglas Tipperman, MSW
6805 Fairfax Road, #123
Bethesda, MD 20814

Safe Place

	Cape Cod, Massachusetts
Mailing Address:	Samaritans "Safe Place"
	Box 65, Academy Lane
	Falmouth, MA 02541

| Contact: | Pamela K. Perry, Box 514 W |
| | Waquoit, MA 02536 |

Safe Place

Greater Lowell and Lawrence,
Massachusetts

Mailing Address:	Judy Astbury
	Safe Place
	10 Apple Blossom Road
	Andover, MA 01810

| Affiliations: | Samaritans of Merrimack Valley |
| | Samaritans, USA |

Suicide Survivors Grief Group

	Edina, Minnesota
Mailing Address:	Roberta Goodrich
	28125 Woodside Road
	Shorewood, MN 55331

Suicide Survivors Grief Groups

	Minneapolis, St. Paul, MN
Mailing Address:	Adina Wrobleski
	5124 Grove Street
	Minneapolis, MN 55436

215

Surviving Suicide   Kansas City, Missouri
   Mailing Address: Jan Olds
                              Surviving Suicide
                              Kansas City Association for Mental
                                  Health
                              1020 E. 63rd Street
                              Kansas City, MO 64110

   Affiliations: Tri-County Community Mental Health
                              Center
                              Comprehensive Mental Health Center
                              Community Mental Health Center South
                              Kansas City Association for Mental
                              Health

SAS–Survivors After Suicide
                              St. Louis, Missouri

   Contact/Phone: Jacque (Stockhausen) (314) 961-0608

   Affiliation: Mental Health Association of St. Louis

Parents of Suicides   The Compassionate Friends
                              Hackensack, New Jersey
   Mailing Address: Parents of Suicides
                              The Compassionate Friends
                              321 Prospect Ave. #F1
                              Hackensack, NJ 07601

   Contact/Phone: Rhoda Payne (201) 343-3908

   Affiliation: Bergen County Chapter, Compassionate
                              Friends

Survivors of Suicide   Madison, New Jersey
   Mailing Address: Joan K. Jaeger
                              9 Linden Lane
                              Kinnelon, NJ 07405

Safe Place
    Mailing Address: Albany, New York
                   Karen Wasby
                   The Samaritans
                   200 Central Ave.
                   Albany, NY 12206

    Affiliation: The Samaritans of Capital District
                   (Branch of National)

Support Survivors
    Mailing Address: Akron, Ohio
                   Sharon Aschelman
                   Support, Inc., Survivors
                   1361 W. Market St.
                   Akron, OH 44313

    Affiliation: Support, Inc.

Suicide Survivors of Widow and Widower's Service
                   Philadelphia, PA
    Mailing Address: Widow and Widower Counseling and
                      Referral Service
                   8001 Roosevelt Blvd.
                   Philadelphia, PA 19152

    Contact/Phone: Dr. M. Rubin (215) 338-9934

    Affiliation: Widow and Widower Counseling and
                   Referral Service

Survivors of Suicide, Inc.
                   Philadelphia, PA
    Mailing Address: Survivors of Suicide, Inc.
                   411 N. Wawaset Rd.
                   West Chester, PA 19382

    Contact/Phone: Ann Clark (215) 431-0122
                   (215) 568-0860, ext. 276

Heartline, Inc.   Spartanburg, South Carolina
    Mailing Address: Heartline, Inc.
                         Drawer A
                         Converse, S.C. 29329

    Contact/Phone: Beth Jones 4617301

Seasons   Salt Lake City, Utah
    Mailing Address: Bonnie Jo Gessel
                         1182 No. 575 West
                         Centerville, Utah 84014

    Contact/Phone: Bonnie Gessel (801) 292-2858

    Affiliation: Seasons: Suicide Bereavement, Inc.

LOSS (Loving Outreach for Survivors of Sudden Death)
                         Edmonton, Alberta, Canada
    Mailing Address: Mrs. Ollie Schulz
                         c/o LOSS
                         13308 91 St.
                         Edmonton, Alberta
                         Canada T5E 3P8

          or: P. O. Box 7303
                         Station "M"
                         Edmonton, Alberta
                         Canada T5E 6C8

    Contact/Phone: Ollie Schulz (403) 476-7035
                         Valerie (403) 476-2835

PROFESSIONAL GROUPS

UNITED STATES

Survivors of Suicide   Huntsville, Alabama
Mailing Address: Joanne Davies, Ex. Dir.
Mental Health Association in Madison
County
P.O. Box 194
Huntsville, AL 35804

Affiliation: Mental Health Association in Madison
County

S/SCOPE—Suicide/Survivors Cope
Birmingham, Alabama
Mailing Address: Tina Akridge
Mental Health Association
3600 8th Avenue South, Suite E-112
Birmingham, AL 35222

Affiliations: American Association of Suicidology
Mental Health Association Crisis
Center

Survivors of Suicide   Anchorage, Alaska
Mailing Address: Marlene Leslie
Suicide Prevention and Crisis Center
2611 Fairbanks St., Suite A
Anchorage, AK 99503

Contact/Phone: Marlene Leslie (907) 272-2496
Gene Johnson (907) 786-1570

Affiliations: American Association of Suicidology
Suicide Prevention and Crisis Center

Ray of Hope, Inc.   Iowa City, Burlington, IA; Joplin, MO
   Mailing Address: Betsy Ross
                       c/o Ray of Hope, Inc.
                       P.O. Box 2323
                       Iowa City, IA 52244

Survivors of Suicide   Contra Costa County, CA
   Mailing Address: Susan Breed
                       Grief Counseling Coordinator
                       Contra Costa Crisis and Suicide
                           Intervention Service
                       P.O. Box 4852
                       Walnut Creek, CA 94596

       Affiliations: American Association of Suicidology
                       C. C. Crisis and Suicide Intervention
                         Service

Survivors of Suicide   Los Angeles, CA
   Mailing Address: Carla Brooke Cowan
                       1026 S. Robertson Blvd.
                       Los Angeles, CA 90035

   Contact/Phone: The Life Clinic (213) 657-6014

       Affiliations: Suicide Prevention Center of Los Angeles
                       American Association of Suicidology

Survivors of Suicide   San Bernardino, CA
   Mailing Address: Susan Kelley Bancroft
                       Suicide and Crisis Intervention Service
                       1669 N. E St.
                       San Bernardino, CA 92405

   Contact/Phone: Sue Kelley Bancroft (714) 886-6730

       Affiliations: American Association of Suicidology
                       Family Service of America
                       Suicide and Crisis Intervention
                         Service/Family Service Association of
                         San Bernardino

San Francisco Suicide Prevention Grief Group

San Francisco, CA

Mailing Address: Lynn A. Ireland
c/o S. F. Suicide Prevention
3940 Geary Blvd.
San Francisco, CA 94110

Survivors of Suicide San Jose, CA

Mailing Address: Director of Suicide and Crisis Service
2220 Moorpack Ave.
San Jose, CA 95030

Contact/Phone: S.O.S. (408) 299-6250

Affiliation: Suicide and Crisis Service

Seasons Grand Junction, CO

Mailing Address: Tallie T. Miller, Director, Grief
Counseling and Education Center
Centennial Plaza, Suite 30
2721 N. 12th St.
Grand Junction, CO 81506

Contact/Phone: Tallie T. Miller (303) 245-6321

Affiliation: Grief Counseling and Education Center
at Stress Management Center

Survivors of Suicide Middletown, CT

Mailing Address: Professor Clayton Hewitt
Middlesex Community College
Middletown, CT 06457

Survivor Group Jacksonville, FL

Mailing Address: Bonnie H. Jacob
Central Crisis Center
2218 Park St.
Jacksonville, FL 32204

Affiliation: Central Crisis Center

Supportive Services to Survivors of Suicide

	Hillsborough County, FL
Mailing Address:	Mary Agresti, Clinical Supervisor
	2214 E. Henry Ave.
	Tampa, FL 33610
Contact/Phone:	Mary Agresti (813) 238-8821
Affiliations:	American Association of Suicidology
	Suicide and Crisis Center of
	Hillsborough County

LOSS (Loving Outreach to Survivors of Suicide)

	Chicago, IL
Mailing Address:	Sheila Dixon, ACSW
	Catholic Charities
	125 N. Des Plaines
	Chicago, IL 60606
Affiliation:	Catholic Charities

Survivors of Suicide

Mailing Address:	Ann Arbor, Washtenaw County, MI
	Jay Callahan
	Psychiatric Emergency Services
	C4050 University Hospital
	Ann Arbor, MI 48109
Contact/Phone:	Jay Callahan (313) 996-4747
Affiliations:	Washtenaw County Community Mental
	Health
	University of Michigan Hospital,
	Department of Psychiatry

Survivors of Suicide

Mailing Address:	Detroit, MI area
	Mary Leonhardi
	Suicide Prevention Center
	220 Bagley, Suite 626
	Detroit, MI 48226
Contact/Phone:	Mary Leonhardi, (313) 224-7000

Affiliations: American Association of Suicidology
Suicide Prevention Center

Friends and Relatives of Victims of Suicide
Westchester County, NY

Mailing Address: Ann Smolin
Westchester Jewish Community Services
83 N. Greeley St.
Chappaqua, NY 10014

Affiliation: Westchester Community Jewish Services

After (All Friends Together)
St. James, Suffolk County, NY

Mailing Address: AFTER
Health House
555 N. Country Rd
St. James, NY 11780

Contact/Phone: T. Musaton (516) 862-6743

Affiliation: Health House

Survivors
Canton, Stark County, OH

Mailing Address: Susan Cross
3421 13th St.
Canton, OH 44708

Associations: American Association of Suicidology
Crisis Intervention Center of Stark
County

Survivors of Suicide Support Group
Upper Bucks, Lehigh, Montgomery
counties, PA

Mailing Address: Ms. Felice Massey
Alliance for Creative Development
1110 West End Blvd.
Quakertown, PA 18951

Affiliation: American Association of Suicidology

The Samaritans   Providence, RI
  Mailing Address: Marion Walters, Ass't. Director
                             The Samaritans
                             33 Chestnut St.
                             Providence, RI 02903

     Affiliation: The Samaritans

Survivors of Suicide   Dallas, TX
  Mailing Address: Steve Hardesty
                             Suicide and Crisis Center
                             Dallas, TX 75204

                             John Tiebout III
                             4209 Lakeside Dr.
                             Dallas, TX 75219

     Affiliations: American Association of Suicidology
                             Suicide and Crisis Center

Survivors of Suicide   Amarillo, Texas Panhandle, TX
  Mailing Address: Esther Quine, Director
                             Suicide Prevention Center
                             Box 3250
                             Amarillo, TX 79106

  Contact/Phone: Suicide Prevention Center
                             (806) 376-4251

     Affiliation: Suicide Prevention Center

Suicide Survivor Support Group
                             Northern Virginia, VA
  Mailing Address: Helen Fitzgerald
                             3601 Devilwood Ct.
                             Fairfax, VA 22030

  Contact/Phone: Helen Fitzgerald (703) 273-3454 (H),
                             (703) 360-6910 (W)

     Affiliations: American Association of Suicidology
                             Mt. Vernon Center for Community
                               Mental Health

Survivors of Suicide   Virginia Beach, VA
    Mailing Address: Leeann Lane-Malbon
                              Tidewater Psychiatric Institute
                              1701 Will-O-Wisp Drive
                              Virginia Beach, VA 23454

        Affiliation: Tidewater Psychiatric Institute

Survivors of Suicide   Kennewick, WA
    Mailing Address: Reverend Kent Selanfelberger
                              7514 W. Yellowstone
                              Kennewick, WA 99336

        Affiliation: Tri-Cities Chaplaincy

Suicide Survivors Support Group
                              Eau Claire, WI
    Mailing Address: Sister Clarita Selz
                              Sacred Heart Hospital
                              Pastoral Care Department
                              Eau Claire, WI 54701

    Contact/Phone: Sister Clarita Selz (715) 839-4121,
                                  834-3176
                              Marjorie Wolter (715) 835-7079

        Affiliations: Pastoral Care Program, Sacred Heart
                                  Hospital
                              Suicide Prevention Center, Dayton, OH

CANADA

Living with Loss   Calgary, Alberta, Canada
    Mailing Address: Cathy Evans
                              Canadian Mental Health Association
                              #201, 723 14 St., N.W.
                              Calgary, Alberta, Canada T2N ND4A4

        Affiliation: Canadian Mental Health Association

Edmonton Suicide Bereavement Program

	Edmonton, Alberta, Canada
Mailing Address:	Anita Marion
	Edmonton Suicide Bereavement Program
	203, 10711 107 Avenue
	Edmonton, Alberta, Canada T5H 0W6
Contact/Phone:	AID Service of Edmonton
	(403) 426-3242, 426-4252
Affiliations:	American Association of Suicidology
	AID Service of Edmonton

Understanding Survivors

	Halifax, Dartmouth, Sackville, Nova
	Scotia, Canada
Mailing Address:	Margaret A. Brock, R.N.
	517 Purcius Cove Rd.
	Halifax, N.S, Canada B3P 2G2

Survivor Support Programme

	Toronto, Ontario, Canada
Mailing Address:	Karen Letofsky, Director
	Survivor Support Programme
	10 Trinity Square
	Toronto, Ontario, Canada M5G 1B1
Affiliation:	Distress Centre

Bereavement Resources Program

	Windsor-Essex County, Ontario, Canada
Mailing Address:	Pat Simone-Mancina
	Canadian Mental Health Association
	Windsor-Essex County Branch
	880 Ouellette Ave., Suite 901
	Windsor, Ontario, Canada N9A 1C7
Contact/Phone:	Pat Simone-Mancina (519) 255-7440
Affiliations:	Canadian Mental Health Association
	Suicide Crisis Intervention Association

St. Patrick's Survivors of Suicide

	Saskatoon, Saskatchewan, Canada
Mailing Address:	Louise M. Dunn
	142 Nesbitt Crescent
	Saskatoon, Saskatchewan
	Canada S7L 6S7

CO-LED GROUPS

Survivors of Suicide	Atlanta, GA
Mailing Address:	Iris Bolton
	The Link Counseling Center
	Atlanta, GA 30328
Affiliation:	The Link Counseling Center

Survivors of Suicide	Topeka, KS
Mailing Address:	Idell Dankert
	Mental Health Association in Shawnee County
	4001 Huntoon
	Topeka, KS 66604
Contact/Phone:	S.O.S. (913) 273-6370
Affiliation:	Mental Health Association of Shawnee County

Survivors of Suicide	Flint, MI
Mailing Address:	Irene Sears
	1309 1/2 N. Stevenson St.
	Flint, MI 48504
Association:	Catholic Social Services of Genesee County

227

Survivors Support Group

	St. Louis City/County, MO
Mailing Address:	Dr. Howard Rosenthal
	Program Director
	Life Crisis Services, Inc.
	1423 S. Bend Blvd.
	St. Louis, MO 63117
Contact/Phone:	Dr. Howard Rosenthal (314) 647-3100
Associations:	American Association of Suicidology
	Life Crisis Services, Inc.

Survivors of Suicide

Mailing Address:	Piscataway, NJ
	Karen Dunne-Maxim, R.N., M.S.
	UMDNJ-Rutgers Community Mental Health Center
	103 Bayard St.
	New Brunswick, NJ 08901
Association:	UMDNJ Rutgers Community Mental Health Center, Rutgers Medical School

Survivors of Suicide

Mailing Address:	Youngstown, OH
	Cathy Grizinski
	Help Hotline, Inc.
	P.O. Box 46
	Youngstown, OH 44501
Contact/Phone:	(216) 747-2696
Affiliations:	American Association of Suicidology
	Help Hotline, Inc.

Survivors of Suicide

Mailing Address:	Memphis, TN
	Mary Sewell, Director
	Crisis Center
	P.O. Box 40068
	Memphis, TN 38104

Seasons   Charlottesville, VA
   Mailing Address: Jean Britt
               138 Harvest Drive
               Charlottesville, VA 22901·

   Contact/Phone: Jean Britt (804) 971-5745
               Juanita Morris (804) 295-2161

   Affiliation: Seasons: Suicide Bereavement

Suicide Survivors Support Group
               Danville, VA
   Mailing Address: Dr. Wasena F. Wright, Jr.
               Mt. Vernon United Methodist Church
               107 W. Main St.
               Danville, VA 24541

               Mrs. L. P. Moss, III
               3089 Country Lane
               Danville, VA 24540

   Contact/Phone: Mrs. Jo Moss (804) 724-4541
               Dr. Wasena F. Wright, Jr. (804) 793-6824

Survivors of Suicide Madison (Dane County), WI
   Mailing Address: Jeanne Adams
               c/o Dane County Mental Health Center
               31 S. Henry
               Madison, WI 53705

   Contact/Phone: S.O.S. (608) 251-2345

   Association: Dane County Mental Health Center

Survivors Helping Survivors
               Milwaukee and Waukesha counties
   Mailing Address: S.E. WAS, St. Luke's Hospital
               2900 W. Oklahoma Ave.
               Milwaukee, WI 53215

   Associations: American Association of Suicidology
               St. Luke's Hospital
               Alverno College

Bibliography

As we have said, many times, there aren't many books to read on the subject of *survivors*. There are too many to read on suicide itself. How to make recommendations, then? First, we chose those books on survivorship that were available and readable; second, a small selection of books on suicide itself that seemed helpful—not medical tracts or analyses of societal ills, but books that might make a survivor's quest for *why?* more fruitful and less self-destructive. Naturally, we have missed some of these, but the bibliographies in other books will probably lead you to them.

Cain, A. C., ed. *Survivors of Suicide*. Springfield, Ill.: Charles, C. Thomas, 1972. [An early entry into the survivor field, this book seems to us most valuable for its historical approach, and for one or two wonderful—if scholarly—articles on the painful aftermath of suicide.]

Fraiberg, Selma. *The Magic Years*. New York: Charles Scribner's Sons, 1959. [An absolutely wonderful book about understanding the problems of childhood.]

Gardner, S. *Teenage Suicide*. New York: J. Messner, 1985. [Offers a few cogent thoughts about the subject.]

Giovaedini, P. L. *The Urge to Die: Why Young People Commit Suicide.* New York: Macmillan, 1981. [For those puzzling the *"why?"* of teenage suicide, a good place to start.]

Grollman, Earl. *Talking About Death: A Dialogue Between Parent and Child.* Boston: Beacon Press, 1967. [Illustrated by a talented artist, this book gives parents a way to talk with children about death that may startle some, help others.]

Grollman, E. A. *Suicide: Prevention, Intervention, Postvention.* Boston: Beacon Press, 1971. [Grollman is a rabbi, and knows whereof he writes; the book is brief, but well written and comforting.]

McIntosh, J. L. *Research on Suicide: A Bibliography.* Westport, Conn.: Greenwood Press, 1985. [McIntosh has been doing research on survivors for some years. This bibliography is invaluable for people who wish to do all the reading themselves. Caution: It's an expensive volume.]

Rudolph, M. *Should the Children Know?* New York: Schocken, 1978. [If anyone still doubts that children should be told about death, this book should dispel their doubts.]

Stengel, Erwin. *Suicide and Attempted Suicide.* New York: Penguin Books, 1964. [Dated in its statistics, this British book is nonetheless valuable for its insight into the relationship between attempted and completed suicides.]

Hewett, J. *After Suicide.* Philadelphia: Westminster Press, 1980. [A paperback book by a clergyman that briefly hits on many of the same topics covered in this volume.]

Wass, H., and C. Coor. *Helping Children Cope With Death.* Washington, D.C.: Hemisphere Publishing Co., 1982. [Not as valuable as Grollman's books, but should be read.]

Webb, Nancy Boyd. "Before and After Suicide: A Preventive Outreach Program for Colleges." In *Suicide and Life-threatening Behavior* 16, no. 4, Winter 1986. Denver: The American Association of Suicidology.

Wilkenfeld, L., ed. *When Children Die.* Dubuque, Iowa: Kendall/Hunt. [This collection of articles is written with the medical and psychiatric profession in mind, but there is some important material here for those who don't mind plodding through difficult material.]

Notes

---

page 5   The source for the list of physical ailments on this page was *Harvard Magazine,* Sept.–Oct. 1983.

page 7   The questionnaire referred to was quoted in a booklet, *The Best of Survivors of Suicide.* Dayton, Ohio: Suicide Prevention Center, 1986.

page 13   Stengel's book is *Suicide and Attempted Suicide.* New York: Penguin Books, 1964.

page 18   The Centers for Disease Control (U.S. Department of Health and Human Services) issued a bulletin in November of 1986, entitled *Youth Suicide Surveillance.* On page 4, they say: "The figures on the number of suicides are based on death certificate data and probably represent a significant degree of misclassification and subsequent underreporting of suicide as a cause of death."

page 21   The American Association of Suicidology, with the aid of some survivor groups, has put out a helpful bulletin—*The Care of the Suicide Survivor*—intended for clergy. There's also one for funeral directors.

page 27   The source for the quote at the top of the page is *The Harvard Medical School Mental Health Letter,* March 1986.

page 28   The *DSM III* is published by the American Psychiatric Association, Washington, D.C.

page 37   Inspiration—and some information—for this section came from Mark I. Solomon's article, "The Bereaved and the Stigma of Suicide," in *Omega: Journal of Death and Dying,* vol. 13, no. 4, 1982–83.

page 40   The physician quoted is Allan Burstein, in a letter to *The New York Times Sunday Magazine,* September 14, 1986.

page 99   The quote is from A. C. Cain and I. Fast, "The Legacy of Suicide," in *Psychiatry* 29: 1966, 406–411.

page 103   The Lindemann and Greer quotation is from chapter 5 of A. C. Cain, ed., *Survivors of Suicide.* Springfield, Ill.: Charles C. Thomas, 1972.

page 112   The quotation is again from A. C. Cain and I. Fast, "The Legacy of Suicide," *Psychiatry* 29: 1966, 406–411.

page 143   Dr. McIntosh was speaking at the first Rutgers conference on suicide survivors.

page 148   The research of psychologist Eugene Gendlin on the self-corrective emotional process that he calls "focusing" and his work on how to help people to focus are the basis for much of what is recommended in chapter 14. Survivors will be interested in his book, *Focusing* (Everest House, 1978).

Gendlin's work has developed out of the work of Carl R. Rogers, whose book, *On Becoming a Person* (Houghton Mifflin, 1961), will also interest survivors.

page 164 *The New York Times* article appeared February 5, 1985.

page 167 The American Academy of Child Psychiatry quotation is from one of a series of one-page flyers the AACP leaves in doctors' offices, especially where children are likely to be patients: *Facts for Families,* volume 1, number 8. The second quotation is from *The Harvard Medical School Mental Health Letter,* March 1986. The third quotation is from T. L. Dorpat, "Psychological Effects of Parental Suicide," chapter 9 in Cain, op. cit. (Some of the ideas in this chapter reflect Dr. Dorpat's thinking as expressed in that chapter.)

page 171 Dr. Fraiberg's book is *The Magic Years.* New York: Charles Scribner's Sons, 1959.

page 179 Nancy Boyd Webb, D.S.W., A.C.S.W., gave us permission to use her ideas about the aftermath of adolescent suicides. Her article is "Before and After Suicide: A Preventive Outreach Program for Colleges," in *Suicide and Life-threatening Behavior* 16, 4, Winter 1986. Denver: The American Association of Suicidology.

Index

abandonment, feelings of, 56, 77–78, 83; in children, 95, 100, 203, 204

accusation, feelings of, 56. *See also* blame assignment; scapegoating

adjustment reactions, 161, 162. *See also* Posttraumatic Stress Disorder

adolescent suicide, 10, 121–31; "cluster" effect of publicity, 25; effects on friends, 179–81; postvention as prevention of, 180; statistics, 179

alcohol abuse by survivors, 40, 92, 101, 103, 114, 140, 198

American Academy of Child Psychiatry, 167

American Association of Suicidology, 5, 41, 180, 209, 211

anger, feelings of, 5, 6, 8, 29, 32–33, 38, 44, 47–49, 56–57, 62–63, 87–88, 93, 104, 112–15, 123, 136, 137, 139–40, 159, 199–200; in children, 169, 175; depression caused by, 39, 138, 140, 142, 169, 202; origins of, 56; relieving, 120, 144; repressed, 59, 60, 65, 83–86, 101, 139, 169; repressed by guilt feelings, 73–78,

82, 86, 140, 169; and scapegoating, 53–54, 65–72, 86

anxiety, feelings of, 6, 38, 40

Babar (children's story), 178

bargains, 8, 53–57, 79, 91–101, 144, 201–5; cutting off, 55, 79–89, 96; defined, 53; family and relationship difficulties, 93–95, 163; guilt as punishment, 55, 73–78, 82, 86; long good-bye, 54, 59–63; scapegoating, 53–54, 65–72, 86; silence, 111–20, 139, 145, 170–71, 198–99; survivor's suicide, 103–10; working to save the world, 97–99

Betti, Ugo, 201

biochemical mental illness, 104, 161

Bipolar Affective Disorder, 79–80, 92, 104, 114, 208

blame assignment, 31, 34, 53–54, 76, 83, 93–94, 106, 111–13, 115, 141. *See also* guilt, feelings of; scapegoating

body, discovery of, 16–17, 141

Cain, Albert C., 98–99, 112

Catholic Church, 34